Job Interview Questions

Java/**J2EE**

Interview Questions
You'll Most Likely Be Asked

355
Interview Questions

Java/**J2EE**
Interview Questions You'll Most Likely Be Asked

ISBN-10: 1-946383-23-6
ISBN-13: 978-1-946383-23-5

Library of Congress Control Number: 2010940415

Table of Contents

This page is intentionally left blank.

Java/J2EE Interview Questions

Review these typical interview questions and think about how you would answer them. Read the answers listed; you will find best possible answers along with strategies and suggestions.

This page is intentionally left blank.

Chapter 1

Architectures and Protocols

1: What is the difference between a Web Server and an Application Server?

Answer:

A Web Server works over the Internet. It uses the HTTP protocol to send the client requests over the Internet on to the server which is located elsewhere and retrieves the information requested from the server or the posts the information sent on the server. ASP, JSP, Servlets, server side Javascript and CGI scripts work for the Web Server. The Web server simply acts as the middle layer passing on the requests or retrieving the requests and provides the HTML page results. It does not involve in any processing or data handling. An Application server provides the business logic to the client using the HTTP or other protocols. The Application server can be a GUI which involves some business logic or data processing programs running on a computer, a web server or other application servers. It exposes the business logic to the client.

2: What all technologies are included in the J2EE architecture?

Answer:

The J2EE architecture includes the following technologies:

a) JAX – RPC which is the Java API for XML based RPC
b) JSP or Java Server Pages
c) EJB or Enterprise Java Beans
d) Java Servlets
e) J2EE Connector Architecture
f) J2EE Management Model
g) J2EE Deployment API
h) JMX or Java Management Extensions
i) J2EE Authorization Contract for Containers
j) JAXR or Java API for XML Registries
k) JMS or Java Message Service
l) JNDI or Java Naming and Directory Interface
m) JTA or Java Transaction API
n) CORBA or the Common Object Request Broker Architecture
o) JDBC which is the Java Data Base Connectivity API

3: What are the benefits of Springs?

Answer:

The Java Spring framework is an open source development framework which can be used to create various sorts of Java Applications including Web Servers. It consists of the JTA, EJB, remote API, JDBC, JMX and JMS which makes the framework perfect for creating all sorts of applications. The Spring framework is a lightweight framework with respect to the size and simplicity. The Spring framework supports Inversion of control which enables loose coupling. It is based on Aspect Oriented Programming or AOP which separates the business logic from the system software. Spring's MVC framework provides a good alternative to other web frameworks. It also provides JTA and Exception handling.

4: Differentiate between SAX and DOM Parsers

Answer:

Both SAX and DOM parsers are used to parse XML documents. The major differences between SAX and DOM parsers are:

a) SAX means Simple API for XML and DOM means Document Object Model.
b) The SAX parser parses the document one node at a time whereas the DOM parser loads the entire document into the memory first and then processes the node.
c) Since the SAX parses on the go, it does not use the memory whereas the DOM uses the memory to store the entire XML document.
d) We cannot modify the XML tree, cannot add or delete nodes in SAX while using DOM we can.

e) SAX supports top to bottom traversing while DOM supports all types of traversing.
f) SAX does not maintain comments while DOM maintains comments
g) SAX parser is faster as it parses node by node and the DOM parser is a little slower since it loads the entire XML document into the memory first and then parses it.

5: What is the difference between a component and a service?

Answer:

A J2EE component is a smaller unit of application software used for a particular purpose. Applets, Servlets, Session beans, Entity beans WAR, JAR and resource adapters are all different components of J2EE. A Service is in J2EE can be considered as the next level to distributed component. It is a component that can be used remotely synchronously or asynchronously. This includes components such as the RPC, Messaging system, Sockets and web services. A service should have a well-defined service contract, is independent and self-contained.

6: What are the design goals of J2EE architecture?

Answer:

The following are the design goals of J2EE architecture:

a) **Service Availability:** The application should be available 24*7. The business depends on the application without the need for customer service representatives

b) **Data Connectivity:** The application should be able to connect to mainframe systems and other legacy systems to ensure business functions as usual
c) **Accessibility:** User should be able to connect the application from anywhere and from any electronic devices
d) **User Interaction:** The user should be able to connect to the application from desktop, laptop, PDA, and mobile
e) **Flexibility:** The architecture should be created in such a way that the developer just concentrates on the business component model (business logic) and the rest of the services are handled by the server

7: What are the roles of J2EE Architect?

Answer:

The following are the roles of J2EE architect:

a) Visualizing the behavior of the system
b) Creating the system blue print
c) Defining the way how the system elements work together
d) Defining non-functional and functional requirements
e) Integrating non-functional requirements into the functional system

8: What is the difference between architecture and design?

Answer:

Architecture defines the structural issues, communication

protocols, data access, synchronization, and subsystems' classification. It also defines the architectural design of the component interfaces.
In Design, we define the components to be created for each interface, the inputs, the outputs, algorithms, and data structures. In short, the designers describe each component's internal details.

9: What are the activities performed in Architectural Analysis?

Answer:

The following activities will be performed in Architectural Analysis:

a) **Use case diagram:** This is developed to depict the high level system functionality
b) **Class Diagram:** This is developed to depict the functionality as classes and methods
c) **Collaboration Diagram:** This is developed to depict how each class talk to each other
d) **Sequence Diagram:** This is developed to depict the operation sequence

10: What are the activities performed in Architectural Design?

Answer:

The following activities will be performed in Architectural Design:

a) The framework (example: Remote Method Invocation)

to be used will be decided

b) The software and hardware requirements are defined
c) The performance parameter and the approach to achieve will be defined
d) Analyze for reusing existing components or technology
e) Define the business logic, security, and performance of the system

11: What are the activities performed in the object oriented design?

Answer:

The following activities will be performed in object oriented design:

a) Decide on how classes interact with packages
b) Create dependency diagrams
c) Create deployment diagrams
d) Decide if the components (software) reside in deployment folder

12: What are the components of multi-tier architecture?

Answer:

The following are the components of multi-tier architecture:

a) **Presentation Tier:** The front end component is present in this tier which is used to display the presentation
b) **Resource Tier:** The back end component is present in this tier which is used to communicate with database
c) **Business Tier:** The component present in this tier is

used to provide business logic for the system

13: What are the advantages of multi-tier client server architecture?

Answer:

The following are the advantages of multi-tier client server architecture:

a) Changes to business logic or user interface can be made independently
b) The client accesses data easily without knowing where data comes from and how many servers available for the system
c) The DB (database) connections can be pooled so that the data can be shared for several users without making DB request for each user
d) The middle tier component (business logic) can be written in any standard programming languages such as C or Java

14: What are the responsibilities of the bean developer?

Answer:

The following are the responsibilities of the bean developer:

a) Write the systems business logic in java
b) Integrate java components with third party components
c) Control access and set transaction parameters
d) Create home interface to find the beans and remote interface to create business logic

e) Create the deployment descriptor xml

15: What are the responsibilities of application assembler?

Answer:

The following are the responsibilities of application assembler:

a) Build presentation layer i.e., user interface
b) Specify the requirements of transaction management
c) Set transaction parameters for all the bean's methods
d) Define security roles and assign permissions
e) Specify wild card character (*) to the methods

16: What are the responsibilities of bean deployer?

Answer:

The following are the responsibilities of bean deployer:

a) Map fields to DB (database) columns and manage persistence
b) Define users, groups, roles, and manage security
c) Use the deployment tools and generate wrapper classes
d) Map user roles and groups
e) Ensure all the deployed bean is assigned a transaction parameter

17: What are the roles of third party software in EJB framework?

Answer:

The third party companies that provide the software can play any of the following three roles:

a) **Component Provider:** Responsible for developing object modeling, programming, architecture, and business process
b) **Container Provider:** Responsible for proving the environment during runtime to the server
c) **Application Server Provider:** Responsible for providing platform to develop distributed applications. It usually contains the container which provides the runtime environment

18: Explain MVC architecture.

Answer:

MVC represents Model View Controller architecture. The activity performed in MVC is explained below:

a) In Model, the developer creates the business logic of the system
b) In View, the developer creates the presentation logic
c) In Controller, the developer receives the request and transfers the response

19: Explain EAR, WAR, and JAR.

Answer:

EAR represents Enterprise Archive file. It contains the components of web, EJB, and client. All the components are packed in a compressed file called .ear file.

WAR represents Web Archive file. It contains all the components related to the web application. All the components are packed in a compressed file called .war file.

JAR represents Java Archive file. It contains all the class files and library files which constitute an API (Application Programming Interface). All the components are packed in a compressed file called .jar file.

20: Explain JTA, JNDI, and JMS.

Answer:

JTA represents Java Transaction API. It is used for coordinating and managing transactions across enterprise information system.

JNDI represents Java Naming Directory Interface. It is used for accessing information from directory services.

JMS represents Java Messaging Service. It is used for receiving and sending messages through messaging systems.

21: Explain EDI.

Answer:

EDI represents Electronic Data Interchange. It is used for exchanging data through Value Added Network (VAN) which acts as the transmission medium.

EDI is expensive to install and requires customization by the exchanging clients. EDI also relies on X12 standards to interchange documents.

22: Explain EAI.

Answer:

EAI represents Enterprise Application Integration. This makes one or more applications as single application and requires data to be transmitted to the appropriate system at the right time.
For example, while integrating sales and account systems, it is necessary for sales to send sales order to accounting to generate invoice. Also, accounting must send an invoice to sales to update data for the sales professionals.
This system handles transaction automatically across application and eliminates human errors.

23: What is the intent for supporting XML in Java?

Answer:

The intent to support XML is to:

a) Ensure Java developers understand XML easier and use XML and XML developers use Java
b) Provide standard for Java to ensure consistent and compatible implementations
c) Ensure java platform can be integrated with high quality

24: What are the protocols used for communicating between business tier and user interface?

Answer:

The following protocols are used for communicating between business tier and user interface:

a) **HTTP:** It denotes 'Hyper Text Transfer Protocol'

b) **JMS:** It denotes 'Java Messaging Service'
c) **RMI:** It denotes 'Remote Method Invocation'
d) **CORBA:** It denotes 'Common Object Request Broker Architecture'
e) **DCOM:** It denotes 'Distributed Component Object Model'

25: What are the advantages and disadvantages of HTTP protocol?

Answer:

The following are the advantages of HTTP protocol:

a) Stateless and firewall friendly
b) Easier to load balance and scale HTTP servers

The following are the disadvantages of HTTP protocol:

a) Difficult to maintain user sessions
b) Limited communication with JSP and servlets

26: Explain JRMP.

Answer:

JRMP represents Java Remote Method Protocol. This is used by Remote Method Invocation (RMI) to pass java objects as arguments.

Since Java relies on Object Serialization which marshal objects as stream, RMI relies on the protocol JRMP to transfer objects from one JVM (Java Virtual Machine) to another.

27: What are the advantages and disadvantages of CORBA?

Answer:

The following are the advantages of CORBA:

a) Supports heterogeneous object
b) Extends the capabilities of ORB (Object Request Broker)

The following are the disadvantages of CORBA:

a) Objects cannot be passed, only arguments can be passed
b) Accepted types of data can only be passed

28: Explain DCOM.

Answer:

DCOM represents Distributed Component Object Model. This uses ORPC (Object Remote Procedure Call) protocol to support remote objects.

ORPC is built on top of RPC (Remote Procedure Call) and interact with runtime services. DCOM supports multiple interfaces and the components can be created in various programming languages. Example of languages are: Java, C, Visual Basic, etc. DCOM is widely used in windows platform.

29: Explain the capabilities of J2EE architecture.

Answer:

The following are the capabilities of J2EE architecture:

a) **Performance:** performs functionality in a short time frame
b) **Scalability:** Supports even if the load on the server increases
c) **Availability:** The system is always accessible across

24*7

d) **Flexibility:** Change in hardware or architecture does not impact the system
e) **Security:** The information cannot be hacked and modified
f) **Reusability:** The component created for a system can be reused and save development time

30: Explain System architecture and Reference architecture.

Answer:

System architecture represents the architecture as product. This comprises the component functions, interfaces of the proposed system, constraints, and interactions. This is the base for application design implementation.
Reference architecture represents architecture as method or style. For a specific domain, reference architecture refers coherent design principle.

This page is intentionally left blank.

Chapter 2

Applicability and Best Practices

31: Explain the best practices to be followed for better performance.

Answer:

The following practices yield in better performance of J2EE applications:

a) Better Resource Management is key to better performance. You can achieve this by creating limited resources, pooling or caching the resources, and by releasing the memory immediately if a particular resource will no longer be used.
b) Minimize the Network Overheads with better design patterns of sessions, EJB, JNDI initial context etc.

c) Minimizing the Serialization Cost by passing by reference and declaring the references as transient.
d) Timeouts make sure that idle objects do not hold the memory for long
e) Applying only the required authorities to the JDBC objects and making sure they are released when not in use will release resources and memory
f) Change the database auto-commit to false
g) Use Virtual Proxy to make sure only the required fields are loaded into the memory as and when required

32: How do Struts, Spring, and Hibernate help improve performance?

Answer:

Struts, Spring, and Hibernate together can help you create optimally designed web applications that are lighter and self-sufficient. Struts take care of the web application framework, Hibernate is an ORM network which forms the database layer and Spring is an Enterprise application framework. If you are building a new application, you can use Spring and Hibernate also since Spring can replace Struts. Spring works on the principles of Inversion of Control and Dependency Injection patterns that guide to better design patterns of J2EE. Struts have an MVC framework with JSP, Servlets, Java Beans, special tags, and messages. Hibernate is portable and is supports mapping of an object to a relational database. It works far better than JDBC is establishing database connections and maintaining transactions. Struts, Spring, and Hibernate when work together provides a better framework of proven design patterns and better connectivity.

33: How does Garbage Collection help in better performance?

Answer:

Garbage collection frees the memory allocated to hold the objects and the data thereby releasing more memory space in the JVM where it can store new objects that are in use. This extra space can be utilized for memory swapping and processing and it is continuous. The JVM uses the stack and heap to clear the obsolete object references and de-allocates them when the program or the code block which has access to the object exits. It is a complicated process wherein the memory is swapped multiple times to make sure the data is available just in case it is referenced anywhere till the point JVM makes sure that it is no longer referenced.

34: Explain Best Practice.

Answer:

Best Practice can be defined as follows:

a) Technique that drives your application design at component level
b) Process recognized by the fellow team members who work on a similar project
c) Takes design or system requirement into consideration
d) Applicable to the entire software development life cycle

35: Explain the J2EE tiers.

Answer:

J2EE has the following tiers:

a) **Client Tier:** It represents the browser from which request is sent to the server. The interfaces used in this tier are HTML browser, java application, an applet, or a non-java application.
b) **Middle Tier:** It comprises of presentation tier, business tier, and integration tier. The user interface is created in the presentation tier using JSP. The business logic is written in the business tier using EJB. The database objects are created in the integration tier.
c) **Backend:** This constitutes the Enterprise Information System (EIS) which is used to store data.

36: What are the best practices to be followed in the presentation layer?

Answer:

The best practices to be followed in the presentation layer are explained below:

a) Separate Hyper Text Markup Language (HTML) from java
b) Always write business logic in a Bean class
c) Use JSP templates and comments
d) Use Model View Controller (MVC) Pattern
e) Use custom libraries and tag handlers

37: What type of components is used in MVC?

Answer:

MVC represents Model View Controller. The component used in Model, View, and Controller is explained below:

a) An application represents the Model which constitutes the system's state. The systems state is created as business logic in a Bean class
b) The user interface represents the View which is created using Java Server Pages
c) The request received from the client is always the controller which is created using Servlets

38: What are the requirements that a J2EE system must possess to operate in a global economy?

Answer:

The J2EE system must possess the following to operate globally:

a) **Financial Considerations:** The method of payment to buy an item should contain many forms as not all the visitors will have a credit card. Also, a government has its own taxes, custom restrictions and tariffs.
b) **Language Requirements:** The application should support multiple languages and it has to be country specific.
c) **Legal Differences:** Customs laws and privacy requirements are different for each country and each government has restrictions on images, ideas, and

speeches.

39: What are the best practices to be followed in DAO?

Answer:

DAO represents Data Access Object. The best practices to be followed in DAO are explained below:

a) DAO should not be coupled tightly to the business logic
b) Each enterprise bean should be associated with a DAO class
c) DAO should be used only to access data from DB
d) DAO should be written in such a way that it allows cross schema and database capability
e) DAO should be written in such a way that it supports portability

40: Explain Guideline.

Answer:

Guideline refers to rule or agreement on operations which are developed by the professionally recognized organization or associations. It also includes approved formal proprietary standards to be followed during the project activities. Example for a Guideline is: Analysts attempting to maximize data content to reduce network traffic.

41: What are the best practices to be followed in VO?

Answer:

VO represents Value Object. The best practices to be followed in Value Objects are explained below:

a) VO should contain business objects with get and set methods
b) VO should update the model bean object with the respective value
c) VO should not reference an object on the server
d) VO should represent a value from the server

42: What are the best practices to be followed in session bean facade?

Answer:

The following are the best practices to be followed in session bean facade:

a) It should reduce remote call to the application server
b) Apply transactional scope to methods which calls entity bean group
c) Simplify the client tier code so that business logic gets executed only on the application server
d) Coding should be done in such a way that it identifies user permissions and provide flexibility and reusability

43: What are the benefits of Model View Controller (MVC)?

Answer:

The following are the benefits of MVC:

a) Separates data model from user interaction and data display and clarifies application design
b) Allows viewing data in many forms and by large

number of users

c) Enhances reusability by separating functionality from presentation
d) Increases flexibility and improves extensibility
e) Encapsulates application functions and facilitates maintenance
f) Supports incremental updates and divides deployment

44: What are the design problems with MVC?

Answer:

The following are the MVC design problems:

a) Components are not aware about the other components' details of implementation
b) Latency issues and communication volumes have to be handled carefully which otherwise result in a scalability issue in distributed systems
c) MVC is difficult to maintain if the Model is unstable because controller is mostly written based on the Model

45: Explain the applicability of MVC.

Answer:

MVC has to be used for the following cases:

a) If the application is large enough and distributed
b) If the application has a longer life time
c) Portability of interface and back end are most important
d) For easy maintenance and reusability
e) Development of application by multiple developers

f) View data and manipulate them in multiple ways

46: Explain the importance of patterns in J2EE framework.

Answer:

Patterns refer to a recurring solution for a business problem in a particular context. Context refers to the situation or environment in which the problem exists. A problem is something that requires investigation and has to be solved and it is specified by cause and effect.

47: Explain Framework patterns.

Answer:

The following are called the Framework patterns:

a) **Proxy pattern:** The EJB remote interface is an example of Proxy pattern. It has methods which delegate method calls to objects

b) **Factory Method:** EJB Home Interface is an example of Factory method. It has an independent reusable class which refers objects through a common interface

c) **Abstract Factory Method:** EJB home interface is an example of abstract factory method. It has a procedure to create abstract class instances from concrete subclasses

d) **Decorator:** EJBObject is an example of Decorator pattern. The functionality of the decorator is that it is visible to the clients

48: What are the activities of a deployer?

Answer:

The deployer performs the following activities:

a) Stage the Enterprise Archive (EAR) file which is created in the development phase into the J2EE application server
b) Modify the deployment descriptor and configure the J2EE application
c) Ensure the Enterprise Archive file (EAR) is well formed and complies with J2EE specification
d) Install or deploy the Enterprise Archive file in the J2EE application server

49: What are the patterns that belong to Integration Tier?

Answer:

The following patterns belong to Integration Tier:

a) **DAO:** The Data Access Object retrieves data sources and delivers transparent data access
b) **Service Activator:** This is utilized for EJB components and supports asynchronous processing

50: Explain Presentation Tier patterns.

Answer:

The following are the Presentation Tier patterns:

a) **Front Controller:** This is used for handling and managing the request from client
b) **Decorating Filter:** This is used for preprocessing and

post processing of a particular request

c) **Composite View:** This is used to create a view from sub components

d) **Dispatch View:** This is used in coordination with Front Controller to view helper patterns and defer activities for viewing the processing

e) **View Helper:** This is used to encapsulate the logic and format the presentation

51: Explain Business Tier patterns.

Answer:

The following are the Business Tier patterns:

a) **Session Facade:** This hides the complexity of business object and centralizes the handling of workflow

b) **Value Object:** This is used to exchange data among different tiers

c) **Service Locator:** This is used to hide the business service creation complexity and lookup. It also locates the service factories

d) **Business delegate:** It is used to separate the service tier and presentation tier, and provides a proxy and façade interface to services

e) **Value Object Assembler:** This is used to build value object from data sources

52: Explain EIS.

Answer:

EIS represents Enterprise Information System. It is present in the Integration tier and supports infrastructure related information for the enterprise.

Accessing EIS is very complex and it requires the following knowledge:

a) Information related to Transaction
b) Information related to Security, and
c) Knowledge on Application Programming Model

53: What are the system level contracts of EIS and application server?

Answer:

The following are the system level contracts of EIS and J2EE application server:

a) The contract 'Connection Management' lets the application and J2EE components to connect to EIS. This leads to a scalable environment and supports many client to get access to EIS
b) The contract 'Transaction Management' supports transaction related access to EIS. This uses the transaction manager to manage transactions
c) The contract 'Security' enables to attain secure access to EIS. This reduces threats to EIS and protects information

54: Explain the Resource Adapter.

Answer:

The resource adapter is the system level contract for Enterprise Information System (EIS). This is utilized by application client or server to connect with EIS.

It collaborates with application server to support security, transaction, and connection pooling. It is used within the application server's address space.

55: Explain data caching.

Answer:

Data caching features are explained below:

a) Caching reduces the network connection trips required for the application
b) It minimizes the shared memory required for the application
c) It reduces the data lookup time
d) It removes memory leaks
e) It ensures caching implemented in development environment simulates deployment or production environment

56: Explain Service locator.

Answer:

To access common services like JMS factories, EJB objects, data sources, etc., which lies within J2EE, service locator is used. The service locator uses Java Naming Directory Interface (JNDI) API which requires initial context object. This lookup the desired service and transfer the same to the requester.

57: Explain how to prevent performance problems.

Answer:

Performance problems can be prevented by the following ways:

a) If the service requires only local access, then never use EJB object but just use java object
b) If you want one bean to access another within the same bean container and Virtual Machine, then use local interfaces
c) Use single remote call and combine all data instead of multiple remote calls
d) Modify unnecessary variable and control serialization
e) To avoid JNDI lookup, cache EJBHome reference

58: Explain a security guideline.

Answer:

The purpose of a security mechanism is to support end-to-end security by integrating existing environments. This process is called Identity management.

Security is handled by creating user accounts in all the application domains and OS (Operating Systems). Also, the security guideline should support authorization and authentication.

Chapter 3

Servlets

59: What are the classes and interfaces used for Servlets?

Answer:

Servlets depend on two packages – javax.servlet and javax.servlet.http. The javax.servlet package holds the interfaces and classes that relate to the details of the lifecycle of the servlet. The javax.servlet.http package holds the interfaces and classes that relate to the http request and responses that sends information and queries to the server and brings the required information from the server. Cookies, sessions and listeners that control the web server connection and its details belong to the javax.servlet.http package, while the init(), service(), and destroy() methods that control the lifecycle of the servlet belong to the javax.servlet package.

60: What is the use of ServletContext() method?

Answer:

The ServletContext() method is used to set and retrieve the initial configuration of the servlet which includes the session, connection and server details. The method returns a ServletConfig object which contains all the initial parameters as set. All application wide servlet parameters are set using the ServletConfig object and the ServletContext() methods returns the object along with the initial parameters set for it. One aspect to be considered is that the Garbage Collector does not de-allocate the memory allocated for the ServletConfig object and hence it has to be handled manually or the object has to be used sparingly to make sure the performance is not affected.

61: Explain the methods in HttpServlet.

Answer:

The HttpServlet is an abstract class that contains the get and post functions to be used over the http server. The developer needs to override these methods to ensure that it works considering the business logic. Since it is an abstract class, the developer must override at least one of the methods and the doGet() method is the one that is usually overridden. Preferably the getLastModified() method should also be overridden to implement caching which further implements smarter conditional GET and the HEAD operations. The other methods available to override are the doPost(), doPut(), doDelete(), init(), destroy(), and the getServletInfo() methods.

Even though the doTrace() and doOptions() methods are also available, they are not overridden. The init() and destroy() methods need to be overridden only if you want to manage the resources.

62: Explain the methods in HttpSession.

Answer:

The HttpSession interface associates the http client to the http server. The sessions store the details on user identity and state which are used across different pages or requests. It contains methods that let the developer set the session values and retrieve the values of the current session.

a) getSessionContext() returns the session context which contains the current session
b) isNew() returns true if the server has opened a new session and the client has not yet joined it
c) getCreationTime() returns the time when the current session was created
d) getId() returns the current session's unique Id

These and more methods are available in the HttpSession interface that provides more information about the current session which is useful in getting to know more about the client. The information is used for validating critical login sessions and how long a user spends time in a website.

63: Can an applet communicate to a servlet? Explain.

Answer:

Applets can definitely communicate to a servlet. It can be done in one of the three ways possible. This can be made possible using a HTTP communication which can be text-based or object-based, Socket communication, or RMI. Whatever the case may be, you need to follow the below-mentioned steps to make the communication possible:

a) First get the server URL
b) Open a connection to the host URL
c) Initialize the connection and set the cache to false, doOutput and doInput to true
d) Create a ByteArrayOutputStream which will store the length of the data to be passed and finally
e) Create the output stream which will actually write the data to the buffer.

64: Will the data in an HTML form refresh automatically when there's a change in the database? Explain.

Answer:

JSP creates pages dynamically. The pages may include html, dhtml, wml or any other markup language. But once the page is generated, it has to be explicitly reloaded to get fresh data even if the database has fresh data. JSP will only have the data which is available when it fetches the same from the database before it is loaded on to the page. But dynamic refreshing can be made possible in other ways such as an explicit page reload which is not recommended as it will involve posting another request and response to the server. It can be done using a

ServerSocket which receives fresh data from the server through an applet which is loaded. But this is also quite expensive as it holds a lot of resources. The easiest way is to use JavaScript to refresh the page at fixed intervals so that it will send a request to the server as in every page refreshes, but here it is done automatically.

65: Differentiate between ServletContext and ServletConfig.

Answer:

The ServletContext interface contains methods that are used to communicate between the servlet and the server container. It handles details regarding the MIME type of the servlet the requests and responses to the server etc. An object of type ServletContext is contained in the ServletConfig object which contains the initial parameters of the servlet. While the ServletContext represents a single Servlet, the ServletConfig is common to all servlets within the JVM, which makes the ServletContext a local parameter and the ServletConfig a global parameter. The getServetConfig() method is used in ServletContext to get the details of the config object. ServletConfig uses the getServletContext() method to get the details of the context object.

66: Which performs better – JSP or Servlet? Explain.

Answer:

Servlets contain the Java components of an application while the JSP is the web component. JSP is used for dynamic web pages wherein the Java code is used within the server tags along with the clientside HTML, JavaScript and CSS codes. The JSP page is compiled into a java servlet class upon the first request. Java Servlets are Java API programs that rest and runs on the serverside. Similar to the JSP pages, when the application requests the servlet for the first time, it is compiled and an instance of the same is kept in the memory of JVM throughout the web application's lifetime. For all incoming requests with a matching URL, the same instance will be used. While the JSP pages use HTTP request and response to communicate with the server, the Servlets use HttpServletRequest and HttpServletResponse for the same.

67: How to make a Servlet thread-safe?

Answer:

By default, Servlets are not thread-safe. So the developer has to explicitly make it thread-safe by adding code. This is required since the variables used in a Servlet are passed by reference and when multiple threads are accessing the same simultaneously the value may be permanently changed. One way you can avoid this is by using a synchronization of a block of code or method which overwrites the value of such parameters. Another efficient method for making the Servlet thread-safe is to implement the SingleThreadModel class. In this case, the servlet engine creates a pool of servlet instances which releases only the available instance when the request is made. Though the response time may increase, it is a more efficient way to make the servlet thread-safe.

68: How to choose among doGet(), doPost and service() methods?

Answer:

The doGet() method is called when the form submits or the browser receives a GET request. The HTML form's method is defined as a GET in this case. When we type in a URL or click on a link, the doGet() method is called. The doPost() is usually called when the form's method is defined as a POST. When we submit a form with data in it, we are actually posting the form. The service() method in the servlet calls either or both the methods as is required and hence, if we are overriding the doGet() and doPost() methods we must leave the service() method as such. The service() method is overridden when the client is using a protocol other than the HTTP to communicate to the servlet.

69: Explain Servlets.

Answer:

Servlets are programs which run on a web server. The purpose of servlets is:

a) Receive / Read the requests sent by client
b) Get information for the request and generate the response
c) Format the response and sent the information to the client

Servlets are not restricted to be used only in web server or application server but they can also be embedded in mail and FTP servers.

70: Explain GET and POST requests of Servlets.

Answer:

The GET and POST requests are handled by doGet and doPost methods respectively. Both the methods take HttpServletRequest and HttpServletResponse as arguments and throws IOException and ServletException.

```
public void doGet(HttpServletRequest myRequest,
    HttpServletResponse myResonse) throws IOException,
    ServletException {
}
public void doPost(HttpServletRequest myRequest,
    HttpServletResponse myResonse) throws IOException,
    ServletException {
}
```

In the case of GET request, all the parameters passed to the server are visible in the browser but in the case of POST request, the parameters are not visible.

71: Explain Servlet life cycle.

Answer:

Servlet life cycle can be explained with the following three methods:

a) **init:** This method is invoked when the servlet is triggered by the web browser. This method creates the instance of the servlet only once and for each subsequent request, the instantiated thread serves the request

b) **service:** This method get the response from the server with the help of the instantiated thread which invokes the doGet or doPost method
c) **destroy:** This method is invoked when the server unloads the servlet

72: Where and how servlets get the initialization parameters?

Answer:

We can define initialization parameters for each servlet in the web.xml file as below:

```
<web-app>
    <servlet>
        <servlet-name>MyMessageServlet</servlet-name>
        <servlet-class>com.message.MessageServlet</servlet-class>
        <init-param>
            <param-name>city</param-name>
            <param-value>Chennai</param-value>
        </init-param>
    </servlet>
</web-app>
```

In Servlet, we can retrieve the value using getInitParameter("city").

73: How can servlet receive the value of html form data?

Answer:

Assume that html form has the following text field:

<input type="text" name="user_name"/>

Servlet can receive form value with the following method:

String username = request.getParameter("user_name");

74: Assume that you don't know the names of the html form fields. Is it possible to retrieve the values in Servlet without knowing the form field names?

Answer:

Yes. It is possible to retrieve all the html form field values without knowing the name of the form fields.

In Servlet, we can use request.getParameterNames() method to retrieve all the form field names and then get the value one by one using request.getParameterValues (parameterName) method.

75: Is it possible to invoke doGet from doPost?

Answer:

Yes. It is possible to invoke doGet method from doPost method. This could be done if the servlet has to handle both GET and POST requests at the same time.

Based on the request type (GET / POST), the service method calls the doPost method which then invokes the doGet method.

76: Explain the syntax of init method.

Answer:

The init method syntax is shown below:

```
public void init() throws ServletException {
    //Code follows...
}
public void init(ServletConfig myConfig) throws ServletException
{
    super.init(myConfig)
    //Code follows...
}
```

So, only from the init method, configuration parameters can be retrieved.

77: What are the advantages of calling doGet method from doPost?

Answer:

The following are the advantages of calling doGet method from doPost method:

a) By default, receive HEAD requests support from doGet method
b) By default, receive OPTIONS requests support from doGet method
c) By default, receive TRACE requests support from doGet method

78: How do you send compressed web pages from Servlet to browser?

Answer:

To send compressed content, first we have to accept the encoding as below:

String myEncoding = request.getHeader("Accept-Encoding");

Then, we have to set the encoding in the browser as below:

response.setHeader("Content-Encoding", "gzip");

This way of displaying compressed contents results in saving lots of download time.

79: Explain status codes.

Answer:

For each HTTP (Hyper Text Transfer Protocol) request, the servlet sends a status code and a message from the server. The status code is a number which represents whether the response from the server is successful or not.

So, if the servlet gets a response from the server, then, in the header, the server will send the status code as 200 and message as OK.

80: Explain the meaning of status code 200 and 404.

Answer:

If the servlet gets a response from the server, then we will get the status code as 200 from the header. By default, the message will be set as OK for the status code 200.

If the servlet is not accessible from the browser or if the servlet does not exist, then the server will set the status code as 404 in the header. By default, the message will be set as File Not Found.

81: Explain sendRedirect method.

Answer:

The sendRedirect method accepts URL (Uniform Resource Locator) as an argument as shown below:

```
response.sendRedirect(myURL)
```

The sendRedirect method forwards the request to the specified URL and is used for redirecting the client from one page to another page.

82: How can we display an error message if a particular page or servlet is not available?

Answer:

If the requested page or servlet or parameter is not available in the server, the server returns the status code as 404.

For example:

```
String myName = request.getParameter("user_name");
If(myName == null)
{
    response.sendError(response.SC_NOT_FOUND, "user_name
    is null"
}
```

In the above code, sendError method is used to send the message to the browser if the value of the parameter is null.

83: What are the methods used to set header values?

Answer:

The following are the methods which are used to set value in the headers:

a) **setContentType:** This method is used by all the servlets which is used to set the type of content (plain / html) to be displayed in the browser

b) **addCookie:** This method is used to insert a cookie in the browser header

c) **sendRedirect:** This method sets the status code as 302 in the browser when the user is redirected to another page

84: What are the values that can be retrieved from the header?

Answer:

The following are the values that can be retrieved from header:

a) **Cookie:** We can get the cookie value available in the header

b) **Content-type:** We can get the type of content displayed in the browser

c) **Content-length:** We can get the length of the content displayed in the browser

d) **Cache-control:** Using this we can identify if the browser content is cached or not

e) **Host:** We can identify the host name and port of the URL from which the response came from

85: Explain MIME.

Answer:

MIME represents Multipurpose Internet Mail Extension. In the header, we will always get the MIME type of the response from the server.

By default, the content type will be text/html in the header when the server sends the response to the browser / client.

86: Explain the most widely used MIME types.

Answer:

The following are the most widely used MIME types:

a) **text/html:** This is used to load content as html in the browser
b) **image/png:** This is used to load png image file in the browser
c) **application/pdf:** This is used to load pdf in the browser
d) **video/mpeg:** This is used to load mpeg video file in the browser
e) **audio/midi:** This is used to load midi audio file in the browser

87: What is a Cookie?

Answer:

Whenever a visitor browses a web page, some information (textual information such as form field values entered by the visitor, book added in the cart, etc.) gets stored in the web browser.

This is useful in the following scenario: If the same visitor visits the page again, the information is served from the browser rather than from the server thereby reducing the server load and time required to load the response.

88: What are the advantages of Cookies?

Answer:

The following are the advantages of cookies:

a) The visitor has to login once and for other subsequent visits, the visitor does not require to login again
b) Identifies the particular user and display the items that were added in the cart
c) Tracks users' interest and displays respective advertisements
d) Reduces the server load
e) Provides faster response to the visitor

89: How can you set and get a cookie?

Answer:

We can add a cookie as mentioned below:

```
Cookie myCookie = new Cookie("name",
request.getParameter("name"));
response.addCookie(myCookie);
```

The above code will add a cookie in myCookie object.

We can retrieve a cookie as mentioned below:

```
Cookie[] myCookies = request.getCookies();
Cookie myCookie = myCookies[0];
System.out.println(myCookie.getValue());
```

The above code retrieves the cookie value from myCookie object.

90: What are the disadvantages of Cookies?

Answer:

The following are the disadvantages of Cookies:

a) When browsing websites from a public computer, cookies store the e-mail address of a visitor thereby allowing others to send spam mails
b) Valuable personal information is stolen by others from cookie objects
c) The sensitive information like credit card details are preserved by cookie which leads to loss of money

So, cookies should not be used to store sensitive information using servlets.

91: What are the options to track visitors browsing a web page?

Answer:

Visitors browsing a web page can be tracked using the following mechanisms:

a) **Cookies:** cookie can be maintained per each page to track the visitors
b) **Hidden Form fields:** Using the input tag, we can store the value entered by the user
c) **URL Rewriting:** In this we can append the data entered by the user to the server
d) **Session:** In this, we can store the value entered by the user in Session

92: How can you store and retrieve a value from session?

Answer:

The value can be stored in session as shown below:

```
HttpSession mySession = request.getSession(true);
session.setValue("mobile", request.getParameter("mobile"));
```

In the above code, the mobile number is stored in the session object 'mobile'.

The value can be retrieved from session as shown below:

```
session.getValue("mobile");
```

In the above code, the mobile number is retrieved from the session object 'mobile'.

93: Explain Session tracking.

Answer:

Session tracking is an excellent technical solution for maintaining user sessions. It uses HttpSession API to look up a session object and create a new session object.

Session tracking is used to store contextual information about the client as the server is not aware about client information. For example, in an online shopping cart, the visitor often add some items to the shopping cart and, suddenly, because of a network issue, he gets disconnected from the web page. Once the network issue is resolved, the visitor will be able to see the items that were added in the shopping cart with the help of session tracking.

Chapter 4

JSP

94: Why should we avoid scriptlets in JSP?

Answer:

Though scriptlets are widely used in JSP, citing the following reasons, they are ideally to be avoided.

a) Readability – The intermittent scriptlet codes in the JSP file are just not readable. At least if the code is written together in one block, that much of code is readable. But the general method of coding followed in JSP is to open and close the script tag wherever required and include the server side logic. This reduces the readability which further affects the maintainability.

b) Maintainability – The code is more than often duplicated to be included in multiple places and it is very difficult to manage the cluttered scriptlet codes spread out in between the client side scripts and HTML.

c) Reusability – The scriptlet codes cannot be reused as they are not written as a named block. This further makes them less replaceable and less Object Oriented.
d) Debuggability – If anything goes wrong in the scriptlet code, the user receives a blank page which makes the scriptlet not debuggable.
e) Testability – Since the scriptlets are spread across the page, it is not suitable for unit-testing.
f) Object Oriented concept gone missing – The scriptlet code is not named under a block and hence they are not inheritable and you cannot apply the principle of composition on them. Hence the basic concepts of Object Oriented programming go missing when we use scriptlets.

95: What do you mean by JSP Compilation?

Answer:

The JSP files are compiled and stored in the memory when the client requests for the page for the first time. You can also pre-compile the JSP files using the jspc command in the Java commandline. The syntax is jspc [options] <file_name>. You can do this when you want to hide the source code from the users. You can pre-compile the final JSP files and these are stored as packages under the jsp package. You can specify various parameters such as the source directory, the destination directory, the name of the failed compilation file as well as the successful compilation file, the target class name of the first JSP and a lot of other options are available along with pre-compilation.

96: What are the life-cycle methods in JSP?

Answer:

There are basically three lifecycle methods in JSP – the jspInit(), jspService() and the jspDestroy(). The jspInit() method is called only once when the JSP page is requested for the first time. It will include all the initial parameters that are required to initialize the communication between the client and the server. The jspService() method is called every time the browser requests for the page and the method accepts the request and response objects as the parameters. The jspDestroy() is called when the JSP instance is no longer required. This is the last method called by the jsp instance.

97: How to set and delete cookies from inside a JSP page?

Answer:

For both setting and deleting a cookie from within a JSP page, the addCookie method of the response object is used. The difference is the setMaxAge() and the setPath() methods that set the to-be-deleted cookie's age to zero and the path to current. The sample code snippet will explain more:

```
<%
// To create a new cookie
Cookie myNewCookie = new Cookie("myName", "myValue");
```

```
response.addCookie(myNewCookie);
//To delete a cookie
Cookie myNewCookie1 = new Cookie("myNewName", null);
//This sets the age of the cookie to zero
myNewCookie1.setMaxAge(0);
myNewCookie1.setPath("/");
response.addCookie(myNewCookie1);
%>
```

98: What is the purpose of JSP?

Answer:

JSP refers to Java Server Pages. It is a server side programming language which enables us to create static html along with dynamic content generation.

Using JSP, we can create the presentation layer to display the contents in the web page with the help of JSP objects and constructs. JSP is widely supported and it can be used with any web server and works in all the operating system without changing the source code.

Developers create a .jsp file which when invoked by the end user from the browser is converted to a servlet behind the scenes. But the end user can just view the html presentation of the content in the web page.

99: What are JSP constructs?

Answer:

To construct a web page, JSP uses the following three constructs:

a) **Scripting elements:** This allows us to specify java code inside the java server pages code
b) **Directives:** This allows us to control the structure of the java server pages
c) **Actions:** This allows us to use the existing components in the java server pages

100: What are scripting elements?

Answer:

Scripting elements are used to insert java code inside java server pages. JSP has three types of scripting elements. They are:

a) **Expressions:** The tag <%= %> is used to define the expressions which is used to display the dynamic output in the web page
b) **Scriplets:** The tag <% %> is used to declare scriplet which is used to define the java code through which we can include dynamic content processing
c) **Declarations:** The tag <%! %> is used to specify declaration which we can use to define java methods which could be called from java server pages

101: What are the most widely used JSP objects?

Answer:

The following are the most widely used JSP objects:

a) **request:** This denotes the HttpServletRequest and is used to create a request to the web server

b) **response:** This denotes HttpServletResponse and is used to generate response to the web browser
c) **session:** This denotes HttpSession which is used to store user specific data in the browser
d) **out:** This denotes PrintWriter which is used to display the content in the browser

102: Explain how to get parameter value in JSP.

Answer:

In JSP, we can get the parameter value by the following line of code:

```
<%
    String strValue = request.getParameter("myParam");
%>
```

So, we use scriplet tag, request object, and getParameter method to get the parameter value.

103: How to display the dynamic parameter value in JSP?

Answer:

In JSP, we can display the dynamic parameter value by the following lines of code:

```
<html>
    <body>
        <%
            String strValue = request.getParameter("myParam");
        %>
        The parameter value is <%= strValue %>.
    </body>
```

</html>

So, we used expression tag <%= %> to display the dynamic parameter value in the web browser.

104: What are the predefined JSP objects other than request, response, session, and out?

Answer:

The following are the predefined JSP objects other than request, response, session, and out:

a) **application:** Using this object, the value of variable is made available to all the servlets (JSP) which exists for an application
b) **page:** This object is a replacement for 'this' and is used to retain the value for a particular page
c) **pageContext:** This object is used to store shared data across multiple pages
d) **config:** Using this object, the value of variable is made available to the particular page

105: Explain JSP directives.

Answer:

JSP directives are used to modify the overall structure of the servlet that results from the JSP page. There are three types of JSP directives. They are:

a) **page:** This is used to import the classes, customize the super class and set the content type
b) **include**: This is used to insert a file into the java server

pages

c) **taglib**: This is used to define custom tags and import the existing tag libraries

106: Explain with an example how to use page directive.

Answer:

The below lines of code depicts how to use page directive :

```
<%@ page import="java.util.ArrayList" %>
<%@ page import="com.core.MyList, com.core.MyVector" %>
<%@ page contentType="text/plain" %>
```

In the above code, we have used the page directive to import java class, custom classes and set the display format of the content type in the browser.

107: Explain the page directive attributes: import, session, buffer, and extends.

Answer:

The page directive attributes: import, session, buffer, and extends are explained below:

a) **import:** This attribute is used to import java class files
b) **session:** This attribute is used to set the session as true or false
c) **buffer:** This attribute is used to set the buffer value in kilobytes
d) **extends:** This attribute is declare the super class in the java server pages

108: Explain the page directive attributes: autoflush, info, errorPage, and isErrorPage.

Answer:

The page directive attributes: autoflush, info, errorPage, and isErrorPage are explained below:

a) **autoflush:** This attribute is used to specify if the output should be automatically flushed or not
b) **info:** This attribute is used to set static values in the java server page
c) **errorPage:** This attribute is used to provide the relative URL of the java server page in case during JSP processing if any exception is thrown
d) **isErrorPage:** This attribute is used to set the value as true or false

109: What is the equivalent XML syntax for page directive?

Answer:

The page directive can be declared in XML as below:

```
<jsp:directive.page import="java.util.ArrayList" />
```

We can use the above line of code in java server pages and it is an XML compatible syntax for page directives.

110: How to display the dynamic parameter value in XML syntax?

Answer:

In JSP, we can display the dynamic parameter value with the help of XML syntax by the following lines of code:

```
<html>
    <body>
        <%
            String strValue = request.getParameter("myParam");
        %>
    The parameter value is
    <jsp:expression>strValue</jsp:expression>.
    </body>
</html>
```

So, we used <jsp:expression> tag to display the dynamic parameter value in the web browser.

111: Explain the 'include' directive with an example.

Answer:

The 'include' directive is used to include a file in the java server pages code. The below lines of code depicts how to use include directive:

```
<%@ include file="header.jsp" %>
```

In the above code, we have used the include directive to include a file which will be processed during runtime and displayed in the browser.

112: What is the equivalent XML syntax for include directive?

Answer:

The 'include' directive can be declared in XML as below:

```
<jsp:include page ="footer.jsp" flush="true" />
```

We can use the above line of code in java server pages and it is an XML compatible syntax for include directive.

113: What is the use of jsp:plugin element?

Answer:

The jsp:plugin element is used to include applets in the web page. It is an alternative to applet tag. The jsp:plugin element can be used as below:

```
<jsp:plugin type="applet" code="HeaderApplet.class"
width="900" height="250">
</jsp:plugin>
```

In the above code, we used four attributes: type, code, width, and height. To display an applet, the value of type should be specified as 'applet' and the value of code should contain the applet name.

114: What is the use of jsp:params element?

Answer:

The jsp:params element is used to pass parameter values to the applet in the web page. The jsp:paarams element can be used as below:

```
<jsp:plugin type="applet" code="HeaderApplet.class"
width="900"  height="250">
    <jsp:params>
        <jsp:param name="MyParam1" value="MyValue1" />
        <jsp:param name="MyParam2" value="MyValue2" />
    </jsp:params>
</jsp:plugin>
```

In the above code, we used jsp:params inside the jsp:plugin element and jsp:param element is used to specify the parameter name and value.

115: What are the important points to be considered while creating a bean class?

Answer:

The following are the important points to be considered while creating a bean class:

a) The bean class should have an empty or zero argument constructor
b) The bean class should not contain public instance variables or fields
c) The bean class should have getter and setter methods to access persistent values

116: How will you include a bean class in JSP?

Answer:

The bean class can be included in JSP as shown below:

```
<jsp:useBean id="service" class="com.MyService" />
```

In the above code, the 'id' attribute is used to create an object 'service' for the class 'MyService'. The above line of code can also be written as shown below:

```
<% com.MyService service = new com.MyService(); %>
```

The class MyService is included in the scriplet and this requires the class to be imported in page directive.

117: How will you set the property value for a bean class?

Answer:

The property value for a bean class can be set in JSP as shown below:

```
<jsp:useBean id="service" class="com.MyService" />
<jsp:setProperty name="service" property="serviceName"
        value="<%= request.getParameter("serviceName") %>" />
```

In the above code, the jsp:setProperty element is used which contains 'property' attribute to specify the bean property name and the name attribute should contain the object name of the bean class.

118: How will you include a tag library in a JSP?

Answer:

The tag library can be included in a JSP as shown below:

```
<%@ taglib uri="servicejsp-taglib.tld" prefix="servicejsp" />
```

In the above line of code, the taglib directive has 2 attributes: uri and prefix. The uri contains the value of the tag library descriptor file in which we specify the class name that will be invoked using the value specified in the prefix attribute. The prefix value denotes the object name of the class that is included in the tag library descriptor.

119: How will you include content of one JSP into another?

Answer:

We have to use the RequestDispatcher class to include the content of one JSP into another. For example, take a look at the below lines of code:

```
String myURL = "/service/transfer.jsp";
RequestDispatcher myDispatcher =
getServletContext.getRequestDispatcher(
```

```
myURL);
```

In the above line of code, the contents of transfer.jsp can be passed to another page using the RequestDispatcher class and invoking getServletContext.getRequestDispatcher method.

120: How will you forward the requests from a JSP page?

Answer:

From a JSP page, we could forward the request as shown below:

```
<jsp:forward page="/service/transfer.jsp" />
```

So, we can use the RequestDisplatcher or jsp:forward element to pass the requests from one page to another page.

121: How will you interpret relative URLs in the destination page?

Answer:

We can interpret relative URLs in the destination page with the below line of code:

```
<link rel=stylesheet href="/css/common.css" type="text/css" >
```

In the above code, the style sheet is included in the destination page using the href attribute in the link element.

122: How will you associate all the properties in the bean class?

Answer:

All the properties in the bean class can be associated with the below line of code:

```
<jsp:setProperty name="service" property="*" />
```

In the above code, * has been supplied for the property attribute to associate all the input parameters available in the bean class.

This page is intentionally left blank.

Chapter 5

EJB

123: Explain the terms "Required", "RequiresNew", "Supports", "NotSupported" and "Mandatory".

Answer:

The terms *Required, RequiresNew, Supports, NotSupported* and *Mandatory* are all used in the context of container managed database transactions using EJB. They are all different attributes that control the scope of the transactions.

a) **Required** – The *required* attribute is the default attribute and it means that the EJB container should create a transaction, if not already there, to execute the EJB method.

b) **RequiresNew** – This attribute suspends the existing transaction, if any, creates a new one and delegates the EJB method call to the new transaction. This ensures that a new transaction is created every time an EJB method is invoked.

c) **Supports** – This attribute invokes a new EJB method within the current transaction of the client. Even if the client does not have an open connection, the method is invoked if the Supports attribute is set.

d) **NotSupported** – This attribute suspends the open transaction the client has before invoking the method, runs the method and then resumes the earlier transaction. If the client does not have an existing transaction, a new transaction is not opened if the NotSupported attribute is set.

e) **Mandatory** – This attribute makes a transaction compulsory for invoking an EJB method. If an existing transaction is not found while invoking the method, the container throws a TransactionRequiredException.

124: Explain fine-grained and coarse-grained interfaces

Answer:

Interfaces become coarse-grained when it contains larger block of components or a set of fine-grained components instead of smaller blocks scattered across the application. Fine-grained components are smaller units of code or data that are connected to each other through relations wherever required. A classic example that differentiates both is the Customer and Account objects. In a coarsely-grained interface, the Customer object will have the details about the account number and the balance too. In a finely-grained interface, the customer details are separate, the address details are separate, the account details are separate and they are all linked by relations.

125: Explain the difference between Session bean and the Entity bean

Answer:

A Java class that implements the Enterprise Bean interface is an Entity Bean. These are generally used to contain the data entities. There are two types of Entity beans – CMP or Container Managed Persistence and BMP or Bean Managed Persistence. The Session Bean can be Stateful or Stateless. The session is established first between the client and the servlet. A Stateful session is one maintains a state between the various method invocations between a client and a server. The Stateless session does not maintain a state between method invocations. The session beans are used to invoke the business methods and logics while the Entity beans are the database objects that actually contain the data. The Entity beans are persistent while the Session beans are transient.

126: What do you know about the EJB Interceptor?

Answer:

Interceptors are methods that have higher preference of invocation than the method being called. Generally, interceptors are used to check and validate the parameters passed or the security checks just before the method is being processed. Another use of an interceptor is to log and profile actions without affecting the rest of the code of EJB. The interceptors can be method level, class level or package level. The default level interceptor applies to all EJBs within the application. It is invoked first in case more than one interceptor is available. The class level interceptor applies to all methods in a class and it has the next preference after the default interceptor. The method level interceptor is invoked just before the method and it has the least preference of the three types of interceptors.

127: Expand and explain ACID.

Answer:

ACID is the acronym for Atomic, Consistent, Isolation and Durable and is the basic qualifier of EJB transactions.

a) **Atomic** – implies that the transaction must either execute all or nothing.
b) **Consistent** – all transactions must be consistent and the developer has to ensure the consistency in transaction level and application level.
c) **Isolation** – a transaction must be allowed to run on its own without any interference from other processes or transactions
d) **Durable** – requires that all data that belong to a transaction are written permanently in a storage system before the transaction is completed. This will ensure that no data is lost.

128: How does EJB help manage the database entity mappings?

Answer:

EJB supports four types of entity relations – one to one, one to many, many to one and many to many. EJB Interceptor annotations are used for mapping the database entity relations. The interceptors are defined in a separate package and included as header files along with the basic java packages included in the main java classes. All database connections and relation mappings are done in the background using Hibernate. Class level and method level interceptors are included wherever required which will do the required mappings and fetch the details from the database.

129: What are the classes / interfaces that must be created for the EJB component?

Answer:

The following are the classes / interfaces that must be created for the EJB (Enterprise Java Bean) component:

a) Home interface (EJBHome)
b) Remote interface (EJBObject)
c) Business logic (bean class)
d) Context objects
e) XML deployment descriptor

130: What are the types of Enterprise Java Beans?

Answer:

There are two types of Enterprise Java Beans. They are:

a) **Session Beans:** This type of bean is created by client and it exists for only one client server session
b) **Entity Beans:** This type of bean is used to represent persistent data which is stored in a database. Each instance of entity bean is identified by the primary key

131: Explain EJBHome interface.

Answer:

EJBHome provides the following three methods for an Enterprise Java Bean:

a) **create():** This method is used by client to create bean instance
b) **remove():** This method is used by client to destroy bean instance
c) **find():** This method is used by client to locate a bean instance and retrieve data from persistent data store

132: Explain EJBObject interface.

Answer:

The access to business methods are provided by the EJBObject interface.

This interface also acts as a wrapper and allows the EJB container to manage and control the object and also intercepts all the method executions invoked on the Enterprise Java Bean.

133: What is deployment descriptor?

Answer:

Deployment descriptor is an XML file (Extensible Markup Language) in which we specify the transactions, security, and persistence details of EJB. In this file, we also specify how each part or component of an application (J2EE) should be deployed.

The EJB container, at runtime, invokes automatically the services as per the values specified in the deployment descriptor.

134: What is a bean class?

Answer:

A bean class is a java class created by the bean developer which contains the business logic implementation methods.

Based on Enterprise Java Bean requirement, the bean class extends javax.ejb.EntityBean or javax.ejb.SessionBean.

135: Explain context object.

Answer:

The context object consists of information about the current state of an instance. The enterprise java bean container use the context object to co-ordinate system services like transactions, security, persistence, etc.,

EJB container generates context object for each EJB instance. SessionBean has SessionContext and the EntityBean has EntityContext.

136: What are the types of session beans?

Answer:

There are two types of session beans. They are

a) **Stateful session bean:** Maintains data state throughout method invocations (business logic), i.e., it maintains session of a particular client
b) **Stateless session bean:** Do not maintain data state throughout method invocations (business logic). This type of bean also utilizes the pooling feature of EJB container

137: What are the methods of remote interfaces?

Answer:

The following are the methods of remote interfaces:

a) **getEJBHome():** Returns a reference to the home interface of session bean
b) **getPrimaryKey():** This method returns session bean objects primary key
c) **gethandle():** Returns a handle for the EJB object
d) **isIdentical():** This method tests if the passed enterprise java bean object is identical to invoked enterprise java bean object
e) **remove():** This method removes a bean (session) object

138: What are the methods of home interfaces?

Answer:

The following are the methods of home interfaces:

a) **getEJBMetaDeta():** This method enables client to get information about enterprise bean
b) **remove(Handle handle):** This removes EJB objects identified by their handles. A handle is retrieved using getHandle() method
c) **remove(Object primaryKey):** This removes EJB objects which are identified by their primary key
d) **getHomeHandle():** This obtains a handle of home object. The client use this object to store a reference to the entity bean's remote home interface

139: What are the services provided by the local and remote interfaces?

Answer:

The following are the services provided by the local and remote interfaces:

a) Returns session object's home interface
b) Removes session object
c) Delegates method invocations on session bean instance
d) Tests if the session object is identical to another session object

140: Explain how a session bean is exposed to the client.

Answer:

A session bean is exposed to the client in the following ways:

a) EJBHome creates instances of session bean and EJBObject

b) EJBObject provides access to methods of session bean
c) The stub acts as proxies to remote EJBObjects
d) The call and dispatch mechanisms are provided by the tie class which binds the proxy to EJBObject

141: Explain local client.

Answer:

The client of session bean is also called as a local client. This local client access the session bean through local (javax.ejb.EJBLocalObject) and local home (javax.ejb.EJBLocalHome) interface.

Local client resides inside the same JVM as session bean and they are location dependent. This local client has objects passed as arguments to the methods by reference.

142: Explain remote client.

Answer:

The client of a session bean is also called as a remote client. The remote client access the session bean through remote (javax.ejb.EJBObject) and remote home (javax.ejb.EJBHome) interface.

The remote client access session bean in an EJB container from CORBA based application which uses remote method invocation Internet Inter ORB Protocol which is a non-java based program.

143: When we have to use EJB?

Answer:

We have to use EJB (Enterprise Java Beans - Session and Entity beans) in the following scenarios:

a) To store client information across method invocations, use stateful session bean
b) For persistent data, use entity bean
c) To communicate the presence of active client to the application server or EJB container, use stateful session bean
d) To invoke the pooling feature of EJB container, use stateless session bean

144: How to manage bean persistence?

Answer:

There are two ways to manage bean persistence. They are:

a) **BMP (Bean Managed Persistence):** In this, we can write a bean class to manage persistence
b) **CMP (Container Managed Persistence):** In this, the container is responsible for managing persistence

145: Explain bean managed persistence.

Answer:

The entity beans implement bean managed persistence. In this scenario, the beans store and retrieve information through direct DB (database) calls.

The entity bean uses JDBC (Java Data Base Connectivity) or SQLJ for storing and retrieving information from data base.

146: Explain container managed persistence.

Answer:

The entity beans implement container managed persistence. In this scenario, the container provides access to the database using standard API's.

The usage of container managed persistence makes the application to use any database. The container also provides tool to map instance variable of an entity bean to call to an underlying DB (database).

147: Explain how will you create home interface of a stateless session bean.

Answer:

The stateless session bean home interface can be created as follows:

```
import javax.ejb.*;
import java.rmi.*;
public interface MYSLSRemoteHome extends EJBHome {
    public MySLSRemote create() throws RemoteException,
    CreateException;
}
```

This interface acts as a factory for EJB objects. The create() method in the bean code corresponds to the ejbCreate() method

148: Explain how will you create remote interface of a stateless session bean.

Answer:

The remote interface for a stateless session bean can be created as follows:

```
import javax.ejb.*;
import java.rmi.*;
public interface MYSLSRemote extends EJBObject {
    public String getMessage() throws RemoteException;
}
```

This interface is used by client when they need to call an EJB object. This interface responsibility is to delegate subsequent calls to the enterprise bean code.

149: Explain InitialContext.

Answer:

InitialContext is a class which acts as a client's interface to JNDI (Java Naming Directory Interface).

InitialContext contains information which allows client to bind naming services like JNDI, CORBA, and DNS. (Domain Naming Service).

If there are problems with InitialContext object or when calling one of its method, then javax.naming.NamingException is thrown.

150: What are the benefits of pooling in EJB container?

Answer:

The following are the benefits of bean pooling in EJB container:

a) Share resources with multiple users
b) We can specify in deployment descriptor the instances

for pooling and for reusing

c) Allows the server (application) to handle multiple requests as the server doesn't have to create and destroy the EJB objects

151: What is the benefit of using DAO between entity bean and data resource?

Answer:

The following are the benefits of using DAO (Data Access Object) between entity bean and data resource:

a) Writes code (entity bean) that is clear and simple
b) Ensures migration is easier to CMP (Container Managed Persistence) for entity beans
c) It has support for other tools with various vendors
d) Provides extra layer for easy communication with data resources
e) It allows cross schema and database portability

152: Explain the role of EJB container in managing entity bean life cycle.

Answer:

The following are the roles of EJB container in managing the entity bean life cycle:

a) Populates pooling with the set of bean instances
b) From the container, client calls create() method of home object and this home object obtains bean instance from the EJB container pool

c) Home object then forwards create() method arguments to ejbCreate() method from the bean class
d) Bean class inserts records into database and returns primary key to the home object
e) Home object returns reference to the remote object to the client and the client invokes business methods from the bean class
f) Then finally the container calls ejbPassivate() method and moves the bean to the pool

153: What are the benefits of CMP?

Answer:

The following are the benefits of CMP (Container Managed Persistence):

a) It has a container specific feature (Example: full text search) for bean provider
b) EJB container also provides support to almost all the existing and popular databases

154: What are the benefits of BMP?

Answer:

The following are the benefits of BMP (Bean Managed Persistence):

a) The entity bean code is container independent, i.e., the code written for a EJB container is portable to other certified EJB container
b) The Enterprise Java Bean and Java Data Base

Connectivity API (Application Programming Interface) can be used for accessing database calls

c) It supports legacy applications and nonstandard data types
d) It also supports various nonstandard SQL servers

155: What are the drawbacks of CMP?

Answer:

The following are the drawbacks of CMP (Container Managed Persistence):

a) **Portability:** There is a chance that the other EJB container portability may be lost
b) **Algorithms:** Container supported persistence algorithm can be used
c) **Efficiency:** The generated SQL is sometimes not efficient when taking performance into account
d) **Access:** The source code developer has no access to view and he / she will not be able to modify the code

156: What are the drawbacks of BMP?

Answer:

The following are the drawbacks of BMP (Bean Managed Persistence):

a) **DB (database) specific:** Since data base specific entity bean is developed, if multiple database access is required, the bean developer have to rewrite the code accordingly

b) **SQL knowledge:** The bean provider must have SQL knowledge

c) **Time:** It requires 5 times longer development time to develop the beans for bean managed persistence

157: How is persistence implemented using BMP?

Answer:

The Bean Managed Persistence is used to implement persistent data with the help of the following two types of methods. They are:

a) **ejbLoad:** This method is used to initiate database communication with the enterprise java bean container

b) **ejbStore:** This method is used to store data using JDBC API's through manual coding

158: Explain finder methods.

Answer:

The finder methods start with the prefix find and it is created in the entity bean home interface.

For example, findByPrimaryKey() is a finder method which is used to identify the entity bean object with the unique primary key object from the home interface.

```
MyRemoteHome myHome = (MyRemoteHome)
javax.rmi.PortableRemoteObject.
    narrow(initialContext.lookup("java:obj/book"),
    MYRemoteHome.class)
Book book = myHome.findByPrimaryKey("91-7822-323-6");
```

The above example demonstrates how findByPrimaryKey is used by bean developer to retrieve data.

159: What are the states of Entity bean life cycle?

Answer:

The following are the states of entity bean life cycle:

a) **Null state:** In this state, the instance of the bean does not exist
b) **Pooled state:** In this state, the instance of the bean exists but it is not associated with any entity bean object
c) **Ready state:** In this state, the instance of the bean is associated with the entity bean object and it has an identity

160: What are the methods invoked by the container during entity bean life cycle?

Answer:

The following methods are invoked during the entity bean life cycle:

a) **ejbActivate():** This method is invoked when the bean instance is ready and associated with the entity bean object from the pool
b) **ejbLoad():** The container use this method to invoke the data from the data source
c) **ejbStore():** This method is used by the container to store data persistently in the data resource
d) **ejbRemove():** The instance associated with the bean is

removed with the help of this method and is invoked from the home interface or remote interface

e) **ejbPassivate():** This method is used by the EJB container to disassociate the bean instance from the EJB object and send to the pool

161: What are the uses of entity beans?

Answer:

The following are the uses of entity beans:

a) To model domain objects with unique identity which are shared by multiple clients
b) To enforce data integrity and persistence
c) To model records in a data source and not to maintain conversations with the client
d) Used either in BMP (Bean Managed Persistence) or in CMP (Container Managed Persistence)
e) To cache data and thereby reuse data and prevent frequent database connections

162: What are the elements specified in the deployment descriptor?

Answer:

The following elements are specified in the deployment descriptor:

a) **session:** Define the bean as session bean instead of entity bean
b) **session-type:** We can define the session as stateless or

stateful

c) **enterprise-beans:** Using this, we can declare the bean as a session bean or as an entity bean
d) **ejb-name:** This is used to specify the unique name for a session or an entity bean
e) **ejb-jar:** This is the root element of the deployment descriptor
f) **ejb-class:** This is used to specify the enterprise bean class
g) **home:** This is used to specify the enterprise bean's home interface
h) **remote:** This is used to specify the enterprise bean's remote interface
i) **transaction-type:** This is used to specify if the transaction is performed by the EJB container or enterprise bean

163: Explain how to create home interface for stateful session bean.

Answer:

We can create home interface for stateful session bean as follows:

```
import java.rmi.*;
import javx.ejb.*;
public interface MySFSRemoteHome extends EJBHome {
    public MYSFSRemote create(int i) throws
        RemoteException, CreateException;
}
```

The create() method in the home interface corresponds to the ejbCreate() method of the bean code.

164: Explain how to create remote interface for stateful session bean.

Answer:

We can create remote interface for stateful session bean as follows:

```
import java.rmi.*;
import javx.ejb.*;
public interface MySFSRemote extends EJBObject {
    public int size() throws RemoteException;
}
```

When the client wants to call an EJB object, they have to use this remote interface. The EJB container is responsible for delegating the call to the actual bean code.

165: Explain how to create a stateful session bean class.

Answer:

We can create stateful session bean class as follows:

```
import javax.ejb.*;
public class MySFSBean implements SessionBean {
    private SessionContext sContext;
    private int iCount;
    public void ejbCreate (int myParam) throws CreateException {
        this.iCount = myParam;
    }
    public void ejbActivate() {}
    public void ejbPassivate() {}
```

```
    public void ejbRemove() {}
    public int size() {
        return iCount;
    }
}
```

In the above code, when the bean is created, the counter is assigned with the parameter value. As per the specification, we have to implement all the methods ejbRemove, ejbActivate, and ejbPassivate along with the business method 'size'.

166: What are accessor methods?

Answer:

When we use container managed persistence, in order to make access to data storage, we don't use direct read and write methods. Instead, we use get and set methods which are called as the accessor methods.

For example getName() and setName(String name) are accessor method for the field 'name'.

167: Explain EntityContext.

Answer:

The entity bean instance is provided by EJB container with the help of EntityContext. The EntityContext provides access to any object reference associated with the entity bean instance including EJB Objects, EJB Local Objects, and primary key objects.

The access to EJB Objects, EJB Local Objects and primary key objects is provided by getEJBObject(), getEJBLocalObject(), and getPrimaryKey() method.

168: Explain getEJBHome, getEJBLocalHome, and getCallerPrinipal methods.

Answer:

getEJBHome(): The remote home interface of the enterprise entity bean is returned by this method.

getEJBLocalHome(): The local home interface of the enterprise entity bean is returned by this method.

getCallerPrincipal(): This method identifies which invokes the bean instance's EJB object.

169: Explain getRollBack, setRollBack, and getUserTransaction methods.

Answer:

getRollBack(): Using this method, we can identify whether the existing transaction for a bean instance has been set as rollback.

setRollBack(): Using this method, we can set the bean instance of a particular transaction outcome as rollback.

getUserTransaction(): This method should not be called by entity bean instances as this method returns javax.transaction.UserTransaction interface.

170: Explain Transaction.

Answer:

Transaction is a task that executes a single unit of work or

atomic operation. If the task is not performed successfully, the transaction will be reverted or rolled back.
Transactions are often referred as ACID acronym. ACID refers to Atomicity, Consistency, Isolation, and Durability.

171: What are the transaction attributes available for container managed transaction?

Answer:

The following are the container managed transaction attributes:

a) **Required:** In this, the container starts a new transaction if the transaction does not exist
b) **RequiresNew:** In this, the container creates new transaction for each method call
c) **Supports:** In this, the bean can execute without transaction
d) **NotSupported:** In this, the bean cannot be invoked with in a transaction
e) **Never:** In this, the bean will never execute a transaction
f) **Mandatory:** In this, each method call requires a transaction context

172: How does container manage multiple transactions?

Answer:

The EJB container manages multiple transactions by the following two ways:

a) The EJB container instantiate multiple instances of enterprise bean thereby allowing database to handle any issues related to transaction processing

b) The EJB container acquires exclusive lock on the enterprise bean instance's database state thereby serializing access to the instance from multiple transactions

173: Explain JTS.

Answer:

JTS refers to Java Transaction Service. It specifies the transaction manager implementation of Java Transaction API (Application Programming Interface).

It supports distributed transactions i.e. multiple database on multiple systems supported by multiple transaction managers. Using JTS, the container makes sure that the transaction can span through multiple containers.

174: What are the services provided by EJB container?

Answer:

EJB container provides the following services:

a) **Transaction Management:** The container manages start, enrollment, rollback, and transaction commitment
b) **Lifecycle Management:** It includes bean creation, destroy, activate and passivate
c) **Persistence:** The beans do not explicitly retrieve or store data from database but do so with the help of container
d) **State Management:** The container automatically manages state of the bean object

e) **Remote Access (Distributed):** The container supports distributed remote access with the help of RMI and IIOP protocols
f) **Security:** The container performs automatically all security checks on behalf of enterprise beans

175: What are the benefits of EJB framework as architecture?

Answer:

The following are the benefits of EJB framework as architecture:

a) The EJB architecture is distributed, scalable, portable, transactional, multi tired, and secure
b) The server for EJB automatically manages services such as threading, lifecycle, transaction, and persistence for the enterprise bean component
c) The enterprise bean components are platform independent i.e. they can be executed on any operating system
d) The EJB components contain only business logic; thereby developers are given freedom to maintain system level code

176: Explain the lifecycle of session bean.

Answer:

The lifecycle of a session bean can be stated as below:

a) Using JNDI (Java Naming Directory Interface) services, the client locates the home object of the bean

b) The home reference is used to create EJBObject which creates the instance of the bean class
c) The bean class called the session bean is allocated a session context
d) The home reference is used to invoke methods on the EJB Object which pass the method calls to the session bean
e) The session bean then returns result to the EJB Object which returns the same to the remote interface

177: What information does the abstract persistence schema contain?

Answer:

The abstract persistence schema contains the following information:

a) For managing each entity bean, it has ejb-name field whose value must be unique
b) For specifying queries, the abstract-schema-name is used for each entity bean whose value must be unique
c) The relationship of ejb can be specified using ejb-relation field
d) To specify the relationship role, we have to use the ejb-relationship-role field

178: What are the types of EJB clients?

Answer:

There are two types of Enterprise Java Bean clients. They are:

a) **Home client:** The home client always exists inside the enterprise java bean container.
b) **Remote client:** The remote client always exist outside the enterprise java bean container

The enterprise bean object can be accessed by multiple clients from the enterprise java bean container through a transaction manager.

Chapter 6

Internationalization and Localization

179: What is Globalization or G11N?

Answer:

Globalization is the methods adopted to make a software product created for a local market ready for a global market. There are many aspects to be considered while making a local product ready for a global market and globalization takes care of those aspects. The focus is on marketing the complete enterprise solution and management support aiming at a global market. The legal and economical factors are given importance here. The terminology, graphics, illustrations, symbols used, colors, character sets, fonts, typography, format, language and style are all to be considered while considering the global market.

180: What is internationalization?

Answer:

Internationalization is the process of making or preparing the code to support multiple languages.

Internationalization involves both application that presents output data to the client and data that can be converted to the appropriate language and character set. So, internationalization allows an application to adapt to a new language and region.

181: What is localization?

Answer:

Localization is adapting to internationalized application which supports a specific language or locale.

Localization involves translating the data into a specific language and maintains it in a file so that the application can access it. The file can be a property file. So, localization provides adaption of an internationalized application to a specific country or region.

182: What is a locale?

Answer:

Locale is an environment that includes locale-specific and regional information. During localization, the internationalized application is adapted to a specific locale.

Each country has its own locale. For example, the US have a

locale en_US and Italy has a locale it_IT and so on. Here, it represents 'language' and IT. Here 'it' represents language Italian and 'IT' represents 'Regional variation' i.e. name of the country, Italy.

183: What are the characteristics of internationalized application?

Answer:

The following are the characteristics of internationalized application:

a) The application will have an .ear file (Enterprise Archive file) which can be executed worldwide
b) The Graphical User Interface labels and messages are not hard-coded within the program but stored outside and retrieved dynamically
c) Dates and currencies appear in end users' region and language
d) To support a new language, re-compilation is not required by the application

184: What are the elements through which a locale is identified?

Answer:

A locale is identified by the following three elements:

a) **Language:** It is the basic identifier for a locale. It contains a valid ISO 639, a 2 letter language code. Each country has one or more language and the language is identified by a two letter word. For example, 'en' for English and 'fr' for French

b) **Regional Variation:** It is the identifier for a country. It contains a valid ISO 3166, a 2 letter country code. For example, FR for France and US for United States of America

c) **Variant:** It is used to create locales with browser specific code. For example, WIN represents Windows and MAC represents Macintosh

185: Is it possible to use java.util package for Localization?

Answer:

We can use java.util.Properties for localization. This class represents a persistent set of properties and it can be saved as a stream. The key name and lookup value in the properties class is a String. For example:

```
Properties appProp = new Properties();
String strProp = "/usr/MyProp.txt"
appProp.load(new BufferedInputStream(new
FileInputStream(strProps));
String serviceValue = System.getproperty("serviceKey");
```

So, in the above code, we have used the Properties file, loaded all the properties and get the serviceKey value from the property file.

186: Explain ResourceBundle.

Answer:

ResourceBundle is a class which belongs to java.util package. It defines a naming convention for locales and it should be used for organizing resources by locale.

Resource Bundle has locale specific objects and it can load the end users locale. So, if we create our own class, we have to use the ResourceBundle class and load locale specific objects.

187: What are the features of ResourceBundle?

Answer:

ResourceBundle has the following features:

a) The content can be localized i.e. the content can be translated into different languages
b) Make the application handle multiple locales simultaneously
c) The application can be modified to support additional locales

188: Explain Character Sets.

Answer:

Character Set is a group of graphical or textual symbols which is mapped to positive integers called code points.

The American Standard Code for Information Interchange (ASCII) character set is used to represent American English. It has lowercase and uppercase alphabets, numerals, punctuation, and symbols. For example, the ASCII code for B is 66.

ASCII was good only for American English. So, in order to

support other languages, ISO 8859 character set was created.

189: Explain Unicode.

Answer:

Unicode defines a universal and standard (ISO 10646) character set. It represents all the character sets that are used around the world and it can be extended. So, Unicode is a replacement for ISO 8859 character set.

Java uses Unicode 2.x for encoding characters. Every character for Unicode uses 2 bytes. Java represents String objects and characters as encoded Unicode. So, programs written in java languages can process data in multiple languages.

190: Explain UTF.

Answer:

UTF represents Unicode Transformation Format. It is an encoding (multi-byte) format that stores characters in 1 byte, 2 and 3 bytes. Here U also represents Universal Character Set (UCS).

UTF is compact and more efficient than Unicode and it is the widely used encoding scheme. Java recommends UTF-8 as it is compatible with the existing web content and also provides access to Unicode character set. UTF-8 denotes 8-bit form of UTF.

191: Explain Collation and Collator.

Answer:

Collation is a process which can sort strings based on locale specific customs. The alphabets are different for different languages and so we need a unique way to Sort strings as per the language. Collation is introduced for this purpose. Collator is an abstract class that belongs to java.text package. This is used for providing locale sensitive String comparison which does the Collation process in Java programming language.

192: What are the attributes used in JSP to control encoding?

Answer:

In JSP, there are two attributes used in page directive to control encoding. They are:

a) **contentType:** In this, we can specify the character set we are going to use and the format of the content
<%@ page contentType="text/html; charset=ISO-8859-1" %>
In the above line of code, we used the html format and ISO-8859 character set of content.

b) **pageEncoding:** In this, we can specify the character set we are going to use for the content display
<%@ page pageEncoding="UTF-8" %>
In the above line of code, we used UTF-8 type of encoding.

193: Explain Format class.

Answer:

Format is a class which belongs to java.text package. It is an

abstract class which is used to format locale information:
Example: messages, dates, and numbers.
Format class uses the format() method:

a) To format locale objects to strings and
b) Parse strings to objects using parseObject() method

194: What are the aspects of the application that have to be varied if they have to be deployed in different locales?

Answer:

The following are the aspects which have to be varied if they have to be deployed in different locales:

a) The presentation of content, numbers, and dates
b) The labels on the components
c) Colors, Sounds, and Images
d) Collation (Ordering) of data presented in the page
e) Reading and Writing text file content

195: What are the font names and font styles supported in Java?

Answer:

The five font names supported in java are: Serif, Sans-serif, Monospaced, Dialog, and DialogInput.
The four font styles supported in java are: bold, italic, plain, and bolditalic. These are the standard names which are mapped to physical fonts that are installed in the operating system by default. The mapping of font names and styles are handled by font.properties.

196: What are the features of java used to create internationalized application?

Answer:

The following are the features of java which are used to create internationalized application:

a) The class java.util.Properties is used to get localized values for the specific text (key)
b) The class java.util.Collator and CollatorKey are used for ordering data based on localized words
c) The class java.text.NumberFormat and DateFormat are used to format currencies, numbers and dates
d) The class java.io.InputStreamReader and OutputStreamWriter for writing and reading files
e) The contentType, pageEncoding, and java.util.Locale attributes are used in JSP
f) The class java.util.ResourceBundle is used for handling localized text

197: What are the subclasses of Format class?

Answer:

The class java.text.Format has three subclasses. They are:

a) **java.text.NumberFormat:** It is used to format currencies and numbers
b) **java.text.DateFormat:** It is used to format time and date
c) **java.text.MessageFormat:** It is used to format text messages

198: Explain why UTF-8 is considered the best encoding choice?

Answer:

UTF-8 is considered the best encoding choice for the following reasons:

a) It is supported by almost all the available web browsers
b) It provides the broadest coverage of character sets
c) It provides efficient data transmission

199: What are the approaches for localizing JSP pages?

Answer:

There are two approaches to localize a JSP page. They are:

a) For each locale, create a JSP file and store it in different directory in the server. Based on the locale of the client request, invoke the respective JSP to display the respective localized content
b) Create one single JSP and use ResourceBundle which has the locale specific custom tags. So, when the client requests a page, the tags access the text from the resource bundle for the respective locale

200: What are the advantages of creating JSP for each locale?

Answer:

The following are the advantages of creating JSP for each locale:

a) **Customization Support:** This provides full support for customizing the structure and display of content for each locale

b) **Clarity in Source file:** All the files properties file, resource bundle, and JSP are kept in one place for each locale

201: Explain I18N and L10N.

Answer:

I18N represents InternationalizatioN where 'I' denotes the starting letter and 18 represents the 18 characters between the starting letter and ending letter and 'N' denotes the ending letter.
L10N represents LocalizatioN where 'L' denotes the starting letter and 10 represents the 10 characters between the starting letter and ending letter and 'N' denotes the ending letter.

202: Explain InputStreamReader.

Answer:

InputStreamReader is a class which belongs to java.io package. It is used to convert byte streams to characters, i.e., it reads bytes and converts them to characters based on the provided encoding.
InputStreamReader class accepts encoding argument as String and converts the bytes to characters. We can identify the encoding type used by InputStreamReader class by using getEncoding() method.

203: Explain OutputStreamWriter.

Answer:

OutputStreamWriter is a class which belongs to java.io package. It is used to convert data from characters to byte streams, i.e., it converts characters based on the provided character encoding.

The write() method calls the encoding converter which converts the available characters. The bytes converted from characters are buffered and written to the output. If the characters do not exist for the particular encoding, then they are substituted with the question mark and displayed in the output.

204: What are the advantages and disadvantages of using ResourceBundle in JSP?

Answer:

The following are the advantages of using ResourceBundle in JSP:

a) **Easy to Maintain:** We need to modify only one JSP to reflect the changes in all the locales
b) **Consistency in Structure of the page:** The page in all the locales follows the same structure and only the data varies for locales
c) **Easy to Extent:** We can easily define a new ResourceBundle which provides support for a new locale

The following are the disadvantages of using ResourceBundle in JSP:

a) **Difficult to customize:** Customizing the page structure for each locale is very difficult

b) **Compatibility:** The page encoding with the encoding of character sets in the application must be compatible

This page is intentionally left blank.

Chapter 7

Design Patterns

205: How do you make sure a class is Singleton? What is the disadvantage of a singleton class?

Answer:

A singleton class is one which allows only one instance to be formed. It either does not have a constructor or has a private constructor and uses the implementation of the getInstance() method to create the only instance possible. You make a class Singleton by following one of the standard patterns such as synchronizing the getInstance() method or by using Enums if you are using a version of Java 5 or latest. Another common method followed is known as eager initialization wherein the class is instantiated at the time of loading whether or not it is used in the program. You can also implement a Singleton Class by instantiating the class inside an exception-handled static block. Thread-safe singleton class can be defined with a synchronized static getInstance() method. Using an Inner Static helper class is also an effective way to implement a singleton class.

The main disadvantage of a Singleton class is that it is not reusable. We can create only one instance of the class. The fact that they do not follow the Single Responsibility principle also works against the Singleton classes. They offer limited flexibility to the programmers and cannot be sub-classed. The synchronized blocks in the Singleton class definition may make the system slower.

206: What are Design Patterns?

Answer:

Design Patterns are procedures for designers which provide solution for a specific problem that exists in a particular context.

Design patterns are used for solving a common problem that comes out during software engineering. It also explains the reason for the problem, the working solution and the reason it is beneficial. With design patterns, it is easy to identify the new problems.

207: What are the benefits of Design Patterns?

Answer:

The following are the benefits of Design Patterns:

a) Focus quickly on the solution for the specific problem

b) Inspire software designers to bring unique and new ideas
c) Real-world problems are solved and provide suggestion for design discussion
d) Domain specific best practices are documented and, thereby, knowledge is captured in the document
e) Defines the circumstances, influences, and resolution of a solution

208: Explain GoF.

Answer:

GoF refers to Gang of Four. It refers to the famous four authors: Ralph Johnson, Richard Helm, John Vlissides and Erich Gamma who wrote the book "Design Patterns: Elements of Reusable Object Oriented Architecture" and published the same in the year 1995. From then on, Design Patterns became more popular.

209: What are the types of Design Patterns?

Answer:

There are three types of Design patterns. They are:

a) **Creational Design Pattern**: These are patterns which are used to create objects
b) **Structural Design Pattern:** These patterns are related to the composition of objects and classes
c) **Behavioral Design Pattern**: These patterns are related to the responsibility and interaction of objects

210: What are the various Creational Design Patterns?

Answer:

The following are the Creational Design Patterns:

a) **Factory Method:** It is the most frequently used pattern
b) **Abstract Factory:** This pattern is used to create a group of more than one type of objects
c) **Builder:** This pattern is another approach to create objects similar to Factory and Abstract Factory
d) **Singleton:** This pattern is one of the most important patterns used frequently by developers
e) **Prototype:** This pattern is comparable to cloning

211: Explain Singleton.

Answer:

The intent of the singleton pattern is to make sure that one class has only one instance and it should be the global point of access. It also ensures that the objects that use the singleton instance always use the same single instance.

```
final public class Singleton {
    private Singleton() {
}
    }
```

The above code illustrates how to create a Singleton class.

212: Explain Factory Method.

Answer:

The intent of the Factory Method is to specify an interface to create an object but allow the subclass to decide the appropriate class to instantiate.

In this pattern, the client will never know the concrete class which is instantiated and which is returned. But the clients need to know only about the abstract interfaces. Some of the interfaces and classes related to Factory Method pattern are:

a) javax.ejb.EJBHome
b) javax.ejb.EJBLocalHome
c) java.text.Collator
d) javax.net.SocketFactory
e) java.net.ContentHandlerFactory

The points a) and b) belong to J2EE and the rest belong to J2SE.

213: Explain Prototype pattern.

Answer:

The intent of the prototype pattern is to define the type of object to be created using prototype instance and create new objects by copying this prototype. This concept is same as the java.lang.Object clone() method.

This pattern allows us to remove or add objects during runtime. It also allows us to define new objects by modifying the existing structure and reduce the need for subclass. This pattern also allows us to configure an application with the classes dynamically.

214: What are the scenarios in which you would create Abstract Factory pattern?

Answer:

The Abstract Factory pattern has to be created for the following scenarios:

a) When the proposed system needs to be independent and does not want to know how the objects are represented, created, and composed
b) When the related objects are intended to be used together by enforcing the constraints
c) When we just want to provide the users only the interfaces and not its implementations

215: What are the various structural design patterns?

Answer:

The following are the various Structural Design Patterns:

a) **Decorator pattern**: This pattern is considered the skin to the guts of Strategy
b) **Composite pattern**: This pattern is used along with Iterator and Interpreter
c) **Proxy pattern**: This pattern is used when controlled access is required
d) **Adapter pattern**: This pattern is used to get access to an incompatible interface
e) **Bridge pattern**: This pattern is used to decouple the main function from implementation
f) **Facade pattern**: This pattern is used to simplify interfaces
g) **Flyweight pattern**: This pattern allows one to utilize

objects efficiently

216: Explain Proxy pattern.

Answer:

The proxy pattern provides a placeholder for an object to control access to another object. The common applications are virtual and remote proxy. Surrogate is the other name for proxy pattern.

In this pattern, the application exists in another workspace but the remote proxy hides this fact. The virtual proxy can create object on demand.

217: What are the benefits of the Facade pattern?

Answer:

The following are the benefits of the facade pattern:

a) Provides simple interface for a complex subsystem and does not minimize the subsystem options
b) It can shield the clients from the subsystem components complexity
c) Promotes loose coupling in between clients and subsystem
d) Each subsystem uses its own façade pattern and, thereby, reducing coupling between subsystems

218: What are the scenarios in which you create Adapter pattern?

Answer:

We use or create the Adapter pattern for the following scenarios:

a) To create a class that is reusable which cooperates with the classes that do not have a compatible interface
b) The object does not have a compatible interface but it wants to use the existing class
c) We don't want to use the interfaces but want to use the existing subclasses

219: Explain composite pattern.

Answer:

The intent of the composite pattern is to allow the clients to execute object that does not represent a hierarchy. This scenario usually appears in a portal application.

This pattern defines hierarchy of classes that contains complex and primitive objects. This makes it easier to add new components. This pattern also provides an interface that could be managed which provides a flexible structure.

220: What are the benefits of Decorator pattern?

Answer:

The following are the benefits of Decorator pattern:

a) This pattern provides more flexibility when compared to static inheritance
b) Helps the developer to simplify code and target classes to develop functionality without coding all the behavior
c) In this pattern, changes are done through coding new

classes and this enhances the extensibility feature

221: What are the various behavioral design patterns?

Answer:

The following are the various Behavioral Design Patterns:

a) **Strategy**: This is one of the most frequently used patterns
b) **Iterator**: This pattern explains how to loop through objects
c) **Template Method:** This pattern helps us to reinforce Factory method and strategy pattern understanding
d) **Mediator:** This pattern acts as a middle tier component
e) **Observer**: This pattern is a pub/sub model
f) **Chain of Responsibility:** This pattern is used to pass messages as a chain
g) **Memento**: This pattern is used to restore and back up the state of an object
h) **Command:** This pattern separates the invoker from the performer
i) **State:** In this pattern, the object changes its class and modifies the behavior
j) **Visitor:** In this pattern, the objects operate on the structure of the elements
k) **Interpreter:** In this pattern, grammar is used to interpret the sentence

222: Explain Strategy pattern.

Answer:

The intent of Strategy pattern is to create a functionality family, encapsulate them, and create them as interchangeable. Here, the functionality is independent from client which uses it. Policy is the other name for Strategy pattern. This pattern provides a substitute for sub classing. This pattern eliminates conditional statements need by defining the behavior within its class.

223: What are the benefits of Mediator pattern?

Answer:

The following are the benefits of Mediator pattern:

a) Provides centralized control
b) The independent components become easier and simpler to develop as they don't need to pass the message in-between
c) The protocols (object) are simplified
d) The components are more generic as they don't contain logic for intercommunication
e) This pattern decouples the other components

224: When will you go for Iterator pattern?

Answer:

We have to use Iterator pattern for the following scenarios:

a) To access collection object without needing to know its representation or internal structure
b) When we want multiple traversal object support in

collection

c) When we want a universal interface to traverse various structures in the collection

225: Explain Interpreter pattern.

Answer:

The intent of interpreter pattern is to define the grammar of a language with an interpreter which is used to interpret the sentence in that language.

Using this pattern, it is easy to extend and change the grammar, and grammar implementation is straightforward. This pattern is used when the efficiency is a high priority.

226: What are the J2EE features associated with the Command pattern?

Answer:

The following are the two J2EE features associated with the Command pattern:

a) Based on the HTTP (Hyper Text Transfer protocol) request type received by the container (web), the JSP or Servlet is invoked
b) Based on the message content dispatched to Message beans, the beans invoke the business logic

227: When will you use Visitor pattern?

Answer:

The Visitor pattern is utilized for the following scenarios:

a) To perform operations on many objects with varying interfaces where the objects depends on the concrete classes
b) To perform unrelated and distinct operations on objects
c) To avoid class cluttering with unrelated operations
d) To define new operations but the structure of the objects rarely changes

228: Explain Template Method.

Answer:

The intent of the Template method pattern is to define the function skeleton and defer steps in subclasses. This lets the subclasses to redefine the function without modifying the function structure. This is performed by the HttpServlet.
This pattern provides a technique to reuse the code and to avoid duplicates. If we want to use the varying algorithm in a subclass and non-varying algorithm in one class, then we have to go for this pattern.

229: Explain Chain of Responsibility.

Answer:

The intent of this pattern is to avoid integrating the sender's request to receiver which is handled by multiple objects. The request is passed as a chain until the object processes the request.
This pattern reduces coupling and improves flexibility when responsibilities are assigned to the objects. It also allows the

group of classes to behave as a single class.

We use this pattern when the request needs to be handled by more than one object and the handler is not known and the request is dynamic.

230: What are the benefits of Memento and State patterns?

Answer:

The following are the benefits of Memento pattern:

a) This pattern preserves the boundaries of the objects that are encapsulated
b) This pattern simplifies the object (originator)
c) The following are the benefits of State pattern
d) The state of the object is local and for each state it partitions the behavior
e) The state of the object transition is always explicit

This page is intentionally left blank

Chapter 8

Messaging

231: What are Messages?

Answer:

Messages refer to unit of data that exists in the local machine or remote machine which can be transferred or shared across network. The data can be a simple text or a complex structure (Example: HashMap).

In the context of Java, by serializing the object, the message can be transformed easily by converting data into bytes, transmitted or shared across network, make a copy of the object, etc.

232: Explain middle tier.

Answer:

Middle tier consists of an application called middleware which provides the following services and business solutions:

a) **Messaging**: It is the ability to receive and send data
b) **Security**: It is the ability to authorize and authenticate user
c) **Naming**: It is the ability to identify the resource by name
d) **Database Management:** It is the ability to access a DB (database) server

233: Explain MOM.

Answer:

MOM refers to Message Oriented Middleware which is mainly used for messaging. It is the infrastructure which enables applications to receive, send, and create messages inside the enterprise.

MOM usually exchanges and delivers messages in different formats reliably and quickly. The advantage of MOM is that it is event driven. There are various messaging vendors:

Example: HP, IBM, BEA, Oracle, etc.

234: Explain synchronous communication.

Answer:

Synchronous communication is the communication method in which the client who made a request is blocked to process any further commands until the requester receives a response.

This communication happens between two parties: client (browser) and server. An example of this type of communication is authorization of credit card. Here, once the card is swiped, the receiver will wait for the response from the server for approval of transaction.

235: Explain asynchronous communication.

Answer:

Asynchronous communication is the communication method in which the client who made a request is never blocked and he /she could continue to work on other process or transaction. An example of asynchronous communication is E-mail. People can send e-mail to you even if you switched off your machine. Once you start your machine, the mail client will load your messages.

236: Explain JMS.

Answer:

JMS refers to Java Messaging Service. It is a middleware which allows the software developers to loosely couple applications. It provides an API (Application Programming Interface) through which we can receive, send, read, and create enterprise system messages.

JMS is a message oriented product which is quite expensive and complex. It provides an interface (Java) to write infrastructure code and allows solutions to be built easily and quickly.

237: What are the message models supported by JMS?

Answer:

Java Messaging Service supports two types of message models. They are:

a) **Publish/subscribe**: In this model, the client can publish a message or subscribe any type of message
b) **PTP:** PTP refers to point-to-point model in which the messages are sent on the basis of one to one

The specification of JMS requires that messaging vendor should support any of the above message models to be complaint.

238: What are the benefits of synchronous messaging?

Answer:

The following are the benefits of synchronous messaging:

a) Synchronous messaging requires two parties (client and server) to be active. If one of the parties is not active, the transaction will not be successful
b) Before proceeding to the next operation or process, the message has to be acknowledged. If not, the message is not considered as processed

239: What are the benefits of asynchronous messaging?

Answer:

The following are the benefits of asynchronous messaging:

a) This type of messaging is not affected much by failures because it does not require or expect acknowledgement
b) This type of message is not affected at the software,

hardware, or at network level

c) Most often, the message is not lost but it might get delayed
d) This messaging works better if traffic increases as it keeps the request backlog in queue

240: What are the scenarios for which we go for asynchronous messaging?

Answer:

The following are the scenarios for which we go for asynchronous messaging:

a) If we do not require the response immediately
b) If we require high volume processing of transaction capability
c) If we want an efficient messaging system to use the hardware system

241: What are the advantages of JMS?

Answer:

The following are the advantages of Java Messaging Service:

a) It provides a way to integrate the incompatible systems easily
b) It supports the asynchronous method of communication
c) It provides support for one or many type of communication
d) It provides support for transactional type of messaging

e) It provides support for guaranteed type of messaging

242: What are the components of JMS?

Answer:

The following are the components of JMS:

a) **Messages**: It refers to the data that is passed between applications which defines the information type the message contains
b) **Clients**: It refers to the application which can receive and send messages
c) **Objects**: It refers to the JMS object which is maintained and created by the admin that are used by the JMS clients
d) **JMS Provider**: It refers to the host application where the JMS application runs. It provides the underlying appliance which is required for the messaging application

243: How are exceptions handled in JMS?

Answer:

JMS uses ExceptionListener interface through which the application is notified if any problem occurs during execution or runtime. This interface identifies the problem details of JMS provider and communicates to the JMS client.

To handle exception, we have to use the onException method which accepts JMSException as argument. This object should register with setExceptionListener method which accepts

Listener as argument in the session.

244: How are messages acknowledged in JMS?

Answer:

Messages are acknowledged in JMS by the following ways:

a) **CLIENT_ACKNOWLEDGE:** The message is acknowledged by the client by calling the acknowledge method
b) **DUPS_OK_ ACKNOWLEDGE:** If the JMS provider fails, duplication of the messages occur. We have to use this only if consumers could tolerate the duplicate messages
c) **AUTO_ ACKNOWLEDGE:** In this, the session acknowledges the client automatically for each message

245: Explain the message headers of JMS.

Answer:

JMS uses the following message headers:

a) **JMSMessageID**: This is used to identify each messages uniquely
b) **JMSPriority**: Priority 9 is highest and 0 is lowest. There is no guarantee that high priority message executes first than the low priority message
c) **JMSDeliveryMode**: This header is used to define the JMS delivery as Persistent or Non-persistent
d) **JMSRedelivered**: This is used to inform client that he or she received the message earlier

e) **JMSExpiration**: This is used to set the message expiration in milliseconds

246: What are the body formats of JMS?

Answer:

The following are the body formats of JMS:

a) **TextMessage**: This is formatted as String and it used to exchange XML data
b) **ByteMessage**: This is used to match legacy messages
c) **ObjectMessage**: This denotes collection of objects or single serializable object
d) **MapMessage**: It is similar to a HashMap which has key value pair
e) **StreamMessage**: This denotes the stream of primitive values that are used to read sequentially

247: What are the types of administered objects in JMS?

Answer:

In JMS, there are two types of administered objects. They are:

a) **Destination:** It contains information that are related to configuration which are supplied by JMS provider. Destination uses queue for PTP and Topic for pub/sub
b) **ConnectionFactory**: It provides the physical connection to the Java Messaging Service through JNDI lookup. It contains IP address and enables JMS to create a connection

248: What are the objects used to receive and create messages in JMS?

Answer:

The following objects are used to receive and create messages in JMS:

a) **MessageConsumer**: This is used to receive messages which are send to a destination
b) **MessageProducer**: This is used to create messages which and send to a destination
c) **MessageSelector**: This is used to filter the message that does not meet the specified criteria
d) **MessageListener**: This is used to process and receive messages asynchronously

249: Explain Message Consumer.

Answer:

MessageConsumer is for receiving messages synchronously or asynchronously to a particular destination which is created by the session object.

In case of synchronous communication, the consumer calls the any one of the methods receive or receiveNoWait and, in the case of asynchronous communication, the client registers MessageListener and starts consumer.

Almost all the messages in Java Messaging Service are exchanged asynchronously among clients where the producer never receives acknowledgement from the consumer.

250: Explain Message Producer.

Answer:

MessageProducer is for sending messages either via PTP or through pub/sub. In PTP (Point-To-Point) model, the destination is known as queue and in pub/sub model, the destination is known as Topic.

In producer, we can set the delivery mode either as NON-PERSISTENT or PERSISTENT using the setDeliveryMode method. Non-Persistent has less overhead as the messages are not logged in the server or database.

We can also use the setPriority method to set the message priority. 0 indicates low priority and 9 indicates high priority.

We can also use setTimeToLive method to mention the life time of the message in milliseconds.

251: Explain Message Selector.

Answer:

MessageSelector belongs to String object which is used to filter the message that does not fit into the specified criteria.

The message selector can examine the header and compares an expression which is present in the String. The example for expression comprises of arithmetic operators, relational operators, string literals, and logical operators.

252: Explain Message Listener.

Answer:

To process messages asynchronously, we have to use

instantiate the MessageListenenr interface. We have to perform the following steps to process and receive messages asynchronously:

a) Create object which implements MessageListener interface and invoke the onMessage method
b) Use setMessageListener method to register with the session object
c) Use Connection object's start method to start receiving messages

253: What are the classes, interfaces, and steps required for PTP communication?

Answer:

The following are the classes, interfaces, and steps required for Point-To-Point communication:

a) Using JNDI (Java Naming Directory Interface) lookup, obtain QueueConnectionFactory object. JNDI name varies based on the messaging vendor
b) Through QueueConnectionFactory object, obtain QueueConnection object. We have to provide username and password if security is enabled
c) Through QueueConnection, obtain QueueSession with provider
d) Through JNDI lookup, obtain queue.
e) Through QueueSession create QueueReceiver or QueueSender for receiving and sending messages
f) Close QueueConnection which closes QueueReceiver,

QueueSender, and QueueSession

254: What are the classes, interfaces, and steps required for Pub/Sub communication?

Answer:

The following are the classes, interfaces, and steps required for Pub/Sub communication:

a) Using JNDI (Java Naming Directory Interface) lookup, obtain TopicConnectionFactory object. JNDI name varies based on the messaging vendor
b) Through TopicConnectionFactory object, obtain TopicConnection object. We have to provide username and password if security is enabled
c) Through TopicConnection, obtain TopicSession with provider
d) Through JNDI lookup, obtain queue
e) Through TopicSession create TopicSubscriber or TopicPublisher for subscribing and publishing messages
f) Close TopicConnection which closes TopicSubscriber, TopicPublisher, and TopicSession

255: Explain MDB.

Answer:

MDB refers to Message Driven Bean. It is a component (stateless) invoked by the container (EJB) whenever the messages arrives in the destination (queue or topic).

MDB is a consumer which receives messages because it implements the interface javax.jms.MessageListener. Similar to a Java Messaging Service, the message driven bean also receives messages in the same manner.

In case of MDB, the Enterprise Java Bean Container ensures that the bean is registered in the particular destination whenever a message is sent.

This page is intentionally left blank.

Chapter 9

Security and Legacy Connectivity

256: What are the various security threats to enterprise resources?

Answer:

The following are the security threats to enterprise resources:

a) **Confidential Information Disclosure**: Accidentally or intentionally making the information available to someone who has no legal rights Information Modification: Accidentally: or intentionally modifying data

b) **Compromise of Accountability**: This is called as identity theft Misappropriation of Protected Resources: This is called as service theft

c) **Misappropriation that compromises availability**: Data modification causes interruption to the enterprise system

257: Explain Authentication and Authorization.

Answer:

Authentication is the process of verifying the credentials of the user who got permission to enter into secured premises or websites. For example, only the registered users are authorized to login in to a website which provides mailing service.

Authorization is the process of verifying the role of the user who got permission to visit or receive the requested resource. For example, the user cannot modify a document because he does not have the role or not authorized to modify a particular document.

258: Explain some of the security packages available in Java.

Answer:

The following are the security packages available in Java:

a) **java.security**: This contains the classes and interfaces for security, authentication, and authorization (access control)
b) **java.security.interfaces**: It contains the interfaces for encryption: Digital Signature Algorithm (DSA) and Rivest, Shamir, Adleman Asymmetric Cipher Algorithm (RSA)
c) **java.security.cer**: It contains the interfaces and classes

for managing and parsing certificates

d) **java.security.spec**: It contains the specification interfaces and classes for DSA, RSA, and Certificates

259: What are the actions performed by Java Security Manger in Applets?

Answer:

The following are the actions performed by Java Security Manager in applets:

a) Delete a file, write a file, and read a file
b) Modify the attribute (Example: priority) of a thread
c) Update or Access the system properties
d) Accept, Wait, or Open a socket or network connection

260: What are the security restrictions in Java applets?

Answer:

The following are the security restrictions in Java applets:

a) a).Applet is not allowed to define native methods or load libraries but it can use its own code
b) It cannot write or read files on the remote or host machine where it executes
c) Network connection is available only to the host machine where it is downloaded
d) It cannot start a program in the host machine
e) It is restricted to read the system properties

261: What are the system properties that applet cannot read?

Answer:

The following are the system properties that an applet is restricted to read:

a) **user.name**: It refers to the account name of the user
b) **user.home**: It refers to the home directory of the user
c) **user.dir**: It refers to the current working directory of the user
d) **java.home**: It refers to the installation directory of java
e) **java.class.path**: It refers to the class path of java

262: What are the policies for access control?

Answer:

The following are the potential policies for access control:

a) Once the user is authenticated, all the processes invoked by the user inherit access to authenticated context
b) Once a component is authenticated, the context is available to all the other trusted components
c) Once the component is ready to impersonate the caller, the caller authenticates the called component

263: What are the authenticated mechanisms supported in J2EE?

Answer:

The web container in J2EE supports the following authentication mechanisms:

a) **HTTP basic**: It contains URL request with parameters

b) **HTTP digest**: It contains URL request with encrypted parameters
c) **FORM based**: This is validated using user name and password
d) **HTTPS mutual**: This allows to perform secured transaction

264: Explain encrypted communication.

Answer:

The data can be encrypted by a mechanism called Cryptography. In this mechanism, the data is encrypted and decrypted using a matching key. There are two types of encryption:

a) **Symmetric:** In this, both receiver and sender know the common key for decrypting and encrypting messages
b) **Asymmetric**: It is called public key cryptography where a key is split into public and private key. Each key has the ability to decrypt data encrypted by other user

265: Explain Digital Certificates.

Answer:

Digital Certificate is the famous solution for private key holder for placing the public key in a package called Digital certificate and sign with a private key of trusted authority called CA (Certificate Authority).

Digital Certificates resolves the public key issue which when received by the party is not trustworthy. VeriSign is the leader in issuing Digital Certificates and the CA is trusted universally and well known. The public keys of VeriSign are distributed with browsers and web servers.

266: Explain Secure Socket Layer.

Answer:

Secured Socket Layer (SSL) is a protocol which ensures privacy on accessing the Internet. These help applications communicate each other so that eavesdropping never occurs.
Secured Socket Layer offers authentication of server, encryption for data and integrity of messages. In SSL, all the data are encrypted and then transmitted across network.
It uses port 443 for transmitting messages across servers. It also uses server and mutual authentication modes to transmit messages.

267: What are the security checks performed by web container?

Answer:

The web container performs the following security checks:

a) Ensures that it has to decrypt the request
b) Ensures that any authorizations constraints are available in the request
c) Ensures that the request contains authorization or authentication requirements
d) The application resources are protected by the combination of authentication and authorization

constraints

268: Explain legacy connectivity using Java.

Answer:

Legacy connectivity approach is based on the client server model which uses two-tier architecture. It is not web based and it uses Enterprise Information System to retrieve and process data.

Enterprise Information System has an adapter which provides API (Application programming Interface) for processing and accessing data and EIS functions. The client uses the API programmatically to connect and access EIS.

The key to Enterprise Information System adapter is reusability. Independent vendors develop adapters using programming language that has high degree of usability and reusability.

269: Explain the authentication in EIS.

Answer:

To access information from Enterprise Information System, the components of J2EE needs to follow a separate security procedure.

The information exists in a protected domain and hence Enterprise Information System layer operates in a separate environment. In this scenario, the container tries to invoke the J2EE components authentication to get the resource. This mechanism is called as container managed resource manager sign on.

270: Explain CSI.

Answer:

CSI refers to Common Secure Interoperability Protocol. The Enterprise Java Bean containers support this protocol and this protocol belongs to Object Management Group (OMG).
CSI v2 is the standard for securing calls over IIOP. IIOP refers to Internet Inter-ORB Protocol. It is the identity assertion mechanism and this feature trusts intermediate entity.

271: Explain EIS adapter.

Answer:

Enterprise Information System has an adapter which provides API (Application programming Interface) for processing and accessing data and EIS functions. The client uses the API programmatically to connect and access EIS.
The key to Enterprise Information System adapter is reusability. Independent vendors develop adapters using programming language that has high degree of usability and reusability.

272: Explain legacy connectivity using J2EE connector.

Answer:

Developers use JDBC (Java Data Base Connectivity) to access data instead of using the approach of using the adapters as this is time consuming. Java Connector Architecture is supported in

almost all the latest servers of WebLogic and WebSphere.
By using Java Connector Architecture (JCA), the Enterprise Information Service (EIS) vendors are not required to customize the adapters for each application server. Also, the application servers need not add code to get connectivity to Enterprise Information System (EIS).

273: Explain Resource Adapter.

Answer:

Resource Adapter refers to implementation of interfaces in javax.resource.spi and javax.resource.cci package. It requires software library in system level when you try to access a resource which uses native libraries to access Enterprise Information System.
Resource adapter by default implements Enterprise Information System adapter of connector system contracts which includes security and transaction management.
The resource adapter also has API at the client level which is used to access the EIS applications. It is also used within the server (application) environment.

274: Explain System contract.

Answer:

System contract is defined as the agreement between two parties to support collaborative and mutually beneficial interaction. For example, EIS and server (application) collaborate to support mechanisms like connection management, security, and transactions.

Using system contract, the component provider focuses on presentation and business logic development for applications. With this, we get a group of functionality from the provider to perform business tasks.

275: Explain the integration strategy of JCA.

Answer:

The major work for developers nowadays is to integrate the new system with the older system. Integration could be performed with the following ways:

a) **Inbound Integration Technique**: In this, the request is initiated by the outside system to our system
b) **Outbound Integration Technique:** In this, the request is initiated by our system to other system

276: What are the types of System Contract?

Answer:

There are three types of system contracts. They are:

a) **Security Management:** This enables the server (application) to connect with EIS using the security related properties
b) **Transaction Management**: This allows propagating transactions from server (application) to EIS
c) **Connection Management**: This describes agreement between container (J2EE) and adapter to establish pooling and tearing down connections

277: What are the ways to configure security properties?

Answer:

The following are the ways to configure security properties:

a) **Principal mapping**: This is used when connecting or combining EIS in the server (application)
b) **Configured Identity**: In this, the resource adapter uses identity connections when connecting to EIS
c) **Credentials mapping**: In this, the credentials of server and EIS are mapped
d) **Caller Impersonation**: This principal used in EIS matches with the application server

278: What are the sections of CCI API?

Answer:

CCI refers to Common Client Interface. CCI API has four sections as mentioned below:

a) **Connection Interface**: This creates connection to Enterprise Information System
b) **Interaction Interface:** commanding execution on EIS is referred to as interaction interface
c) **ResultSet Interface**: This encapsulates query results to EIS
d) **Metadata Interface:** This allows to examine EIS metadata

279: Explain ManagedConnectionFactory and ManagedConnection.

Answer:

ManagedConnectionFactory is an interface which is implemented by the class UCManagedConnectionFactory (Entry point for the server to call adapter) which creates the UCConnectionFactory and UCManagedConnection class. ManagedConnection is an interface which is implemented by the UCManagedConnection class. This class encapsulates adapters connection (physical) class UCConnection.

Both ManagedConnectionFactory and ManagedConnection are used for implanting JCA (Java Connector Architecture) adapter.

280: What are the drawbacks of DB integrity constraints?

Answer:

The following are the drawbacks of DB (Data Base) integrity constraints:

a) **Logic Duplication:** The logic duplication is possible when the database integrity rules are changed which requires change in business logic code
b) **DBMS constraints non-portability:** Using procedural triggers often leads to non-portability as each vendor follows their own standards
c) **Uncontrolled DB configuration:** Since the constraints exists outside server (J2EE), configurations are performed with the DB vendor tools

HR Questions

Review these typical interview questions and think about how you would answer them. Read the answers listed; you will find best possible answers along with strategies and suggestions.

1: Tell me about a time when you didn't meet a deadline.

Answer:

Ideally, this hasn't happened – but if it has, make sure you use a minor example to illustrate the situation, emphasize how long ago it happened, and be sure that you did as much as you could to ensure that the deadline was met. Additionally, be sure to include what you learned about managing time better or prioritizing tasks in order to meet all future deadlines.

2: How do you eliminate distractions while working?

Answer:

With the increase of technology and the ease of communication, new distractions arise every day. Your interviewer will want to see that you are still able to focus on work, and that your productivity has not been affected, by an example showing a routine you employ in order to stay on task.

3: Tell me about a time when you worked in a position with a weekly or monthly quota to meet. How often were you successful?

Answer:

Your numbers will speak for themselves, and you must answer this question honestly. If you were regularly met your quotas, be sure to highlight this in a confident manner and don't be shy in pointing out your strengths in this area. If your statistics are less than stellar, try to point out trends in which they increased toward the end of your employment, and show reflection as to ways you can improve in the future.

4: Tell me about a time when you met a tough deadline, and how you were able to complete it.

Answer:

Explain how you were able to prioritize tasks, or to delegate portions of an assignments to other team members, in order to deal with a tough deadline. It may be beneficial to specify why the deadline was tough – make sure it's clear that it was not a result of procrastination on your part. Finally, explain how you were able to successfully meet the deadline, and what it took to get there in the end.

5: How do you stay organized when you have multiple projects on your plate?

Answer:

The interviewer will be looking to see that you can manage your time and work well – and being able to handle multiple projects at once, and still giving each the attention it deserves, is a great mark of a worker's competence and efficiency. Go through a typical process of goal-setting and prioritizing, and explain the steps of these to the interviewer, so he or she can see how well you manage time.

6: How much time during your work day do you spend on "auto-pilot?"

Answer:

While you may wonder if the employer is looking to see how efficient you are with this question (for example, so good at your job that you don't have to think about it), but in almost every case, the employer wants to see that you're constantly thinking, analyzing, and processing what's going on in the workplace. Even if things are running smoothly, there's usually an opportunity somewhere to make things more efficient or to increase sales or productivity. Stress your dedication to ongoing development, and convey that being on "auto-pilot" is not conducive to that type of success.

7: How do you handle deadlines?

Answer:

The most important part of handling tough deadlines is to prioritize tasks and set goals for completion, as well as to delegate or eliminate unnecessary work. Lead the interviewer through a general scenario, and display your competency through your ability to organize and set priorities, and most importantly, remain calm.

8: Tell me about your personal problem-solving process.

Answer:

Your personal problem-solving process should include outlining the problem, coming up with possible ways to fix the problem, and setting a clear action plan that leads to resolution. Keep your answer brief and organized, and explain the steps in a concise, calm manner that shows you are level-headed even under stress.

9: What sort of things at work can make you stressed?

Answer:

As it's best to stay away from negatives, keep this answer brief and simple. While answering that nothing at work makes you stressed will not be very believable to the interviewer, keep your answer to one generic principle such as when members of a team don't keep their commitments, and then focus on a solution you generally employ to tackle that stress, such as having weekly status meetings or intermittent deadlines along the course of a project.

10: What do you look like when you are stressed about something? How do you solve it?

Answer:

This is a trick question – your interviewer wants to hear that you don't look any different when you're stressed, and that you don't allow negative emotions to interfere with your productivity. As far as how you solve your stress, it's best if you have a simple solution mastered, such as simply taking deep breaths and counting to 10 to bring yourself back to the task at hand.

11: Can you multi-task?

Answer:

Some people can, and some people can't. The most important part of multi-tasking is to keep a clear head at all times about what needs to be done, and what priority each task falls under. Explain how you evaluate tasks to determine priority, and how you manage your time in order to ensure that all are completed efficiently.

12: How many hours per week do you work?

Answer:

Many people get tricked by this question, thinking that answering more hours is better – however, this may cause an employer to wonder why you have to work so many hours in order to get the work done that other people can do in a shorter amount of time. Give a fair estimate of hours that it should take you to complete a job, and explain that you are also willing to work extra whenever needed.

13: How many times per day do you check your email?

Answer:

While an employer wants to see that you are plugged into modern technology, it is also important that the number of times you check your email per day is relatively low – perhaps two to three times per day (dependent on the specific field you're in). Checking email is often a great distraction in the workplace, and while it is important to remain connected, much correspondence can simply be handled together in the morning and afternoon.

14: What has been your biggest success?

Answer:

Your biggest success should be something that was especially meaningful to you, and that you can talk about passionately – your interviewer will be able to see this. Always have an answer prepared for this question, and be sure to explain how you achieved success, as well as what you learned from the experience.

15: What motivates you?

Answer:

It's best to focus on a key aspect of your work that you can target as a "driving force" behind your everyday work. Whether it's customer service, making a difference, or the chance to further your skills and gain experience, it's important that the interviewer can see the passion you hold for your career and the dedication you have to the position.

16: What do you do when you lose motivation?

Answer:

The best candidates will answer that they rarely lose motivation, because they already employ strategies to keep themselves inspired, and because they remain dedicated to their objectives. Additionally, you may impress the interviewer by explaining that you are motivated by achieving goals and advancing, so small successes are always a great way to regain momentum.

17: What do you like to do in your free time?

Answer:

What you do answer here is not nearly as important as what you don't answer – your interviewer does not want to hear that you like to drink, party, or revel in the nightlife. Instead, choose a few activities to focus on that are greater signs of stability and maturity, and that will not detract from your ability to show up to work and be productive, such as reading, cooking, or photography. This is also a great opportunity to show your interviewer that you are a well-rounded, interesting, and dynamic personality that they would be happy to hire.

18: What sets you apart from other workers?

Answer:

This question is a great opportunity to highlight the specific skill sets and passion you bring to the company that no one else can. If you can't outline exactly what sets you apart from other workers, how will the interviewer see it? Be prepared with a thorough outline of what you will bring to the table, in order to help the company achieve their goals.

19: Why are you the best candidate for that position?

Answer:

Have a brief response prepared in advance for this question, as this is another very common theme in interviews (variations of the question include: "Why should I hire you, above Candidate

B?" and "What can you bring to our company that Candidate B cannot?"). Make sure that your statement does not sound rehearsed, and highlight your most unique qualities that show the interviewer why he or she must hire you above all the other candidates. Include specific details about your experience and special projects or recognition you've received that set you apart, and show your greatest passion, commitment, and enthusiasm for the position.

20: What does it take to be successful?

Answer:

Hard work, passion, motivation, and a dedication to learning – these are all potential answers to the ambiguous concept of success. It doesn't matter so much which of these values you choose as the primary means to success, or if you choose a combination of them. It is, however, absolutely key that whichever value you choose, you must clearly display in your attitude, experience, and goals.

21: What would be the biggest challenge in this position for you?

Answer:

Keep this answer positive, and remain focused on the opportunities for growth and learning that the position can provide. Be sure that no matter what the challenge is, it's obvious that you're ready and enthusiastic to tackle it, and that you have a full awareness of what it will take to get the job done.

22: Would you describe yourself as an introvert or an extrovert?

Answer:

There are beneficial qualities to each of these, and your answer may depend on what type of work you're involved in. However, a successful leader may be an introvert or extrovert, and similarly, solid team members may also be either. The important aspect of this question is to have the level of self-awareness required to accurately describe yourself.

23: What are some positive character traits that you don't possess?

Answer:

If an interviewer asks you a tough question about your weaknesses, or lack of positive traits, it's best to keep your answer light-hearted and simple – for instance, express your great confidence in your own abilities, followed by a (rather humble) admittance that you could occasionally do to be more humble.

24: What is the greatest lesson you've ever learned?

Answer:

While this is a very broad question, the interviewer will be more interested in hearing what kind of emphasis you place on this value. Your greatest lesson may tie in with something a mentor, parent, or professor once told you, or you may have gleaned it from a book written by a leading expert in your field. Regardless of what the lesson is, it is most important that you can offer an example of how you've incorporated it into your life.

25: Have you ever been in a situation where one of your strengths became a weakness in an alternate setting?

Answer:

It's important to show an awareness of yourself by having an answer for this question, but you want to make sure that the weakness is relatively minor, and that it would still remain a strength in most settings. For instance, you may be an avid reader who reads anything and everything you can find, but reading billboards while driving to work may be a dangerous idea.

26: Who has been the most influential person in your life?

Answer:

Give a specific example (and name) to the person who has influenced your life greatly, and offer a relevant anecdote about a meaningful exchange the two of you shared. It's great if their influence relates to your professional life, but this particular question opens up the possibility to discuss inspiration in your personal life as well. The interviewer wants to see that you're able to make strong connections with other individuals, and to work under the guiding influence of another person.

27: Do you consider yourself to be a "detailed" or "big picture" type of person?

Answer:

Both of these are great qualities, and it's best if you can incorporate each into your answer. Choose one as your primary type, and relate it to experience or specific items from your resume. Then, explain how the other type fits into your work as well.

28: What is your greatest fear?

Answer:

Disclosing your greatest fear openly and without embarrassment is a great way to show your confidence to an employer. Choose a fear that you are clearly doing work to combat, such as a fear of failure that will seem impossible to the interviewer for someone such as yourself, with such clear goals and actions plans outlined. As tempting as it may be to stick with an easy answer such as spiders, stay away from these, as they don't really tell the interviewer anything about yourself that's relevant.

29: What sort of challenges do you enjoy?

Answer:

The challenges you enjoy should demonstrate some sort of initiative or growth potential on your part, and should also be in line with your career objectives. Employers will evaluate consistency here, as they analyze critically how the challenges you look forward to are related to your ultimate goals.

30: Tell me about a time you were embarrassed. How did you handle it?

Answer:

No one wants to bring up times they were embarrassed in a job interview, and it's probably best to avoid an anecdote here. However, don't shy away from offering a brief synopsis, followed by a display of your ability to laugh it off. Show the interviewer that it was not an event that impacted you significantly.

31: What is your greatest weakness?

Answer:

This is another one of the most popular questions asked in job interviews, so you should be prepared with an answer already. Try to come up with a weakness that you have that can actually be a strength in an alternate setting – such as, "I'm very detail-oriented and like to ensure that things are done correctly, so I sometimes have difficulty in delegating tasks to others." However, don't try to mask obvious weaknesses – if you have little practical experience in the field, mention that you're looking forward to great opportunities to further your knowledge.

32: What are the three best adjectives to describe you in a work setting?

Answer:

While these three adjectives probably already appear somewhere on your resume, don't be afraid to use them again in order to highlight your best qualities. This is a chance for you to sell yourself to the interviewer, and to point out traits you possess that other candidates do not. Use the most specific and accurate words you can think of, and elaborate shortly on how you embody each.

33: What are the three best adjectives to describe you in your personal life?

Answer:

Ideally, the three adjectives that describe you in your personal life should be similar to the adjectives that describe you in your professional life. Employers appreciate consistency, and while they may be understanding of you having an alternate personality outside of the office, it's best if you employ similar principles in your actions both on and off the clock.

34: What type of worker are you?

Answer:

This is an opportunity for you to highlight some of your greatest assets. Characterize some of your talents such as dedicated, self-motivated, detail-oriented, passionate, hard-working, analytical, or customer service focused. Stay away from your weaker qualities here, and remain on the target of all the wonderful things that you can bring to the company.

35: Tell me about your happiest day at work.

Answer:

Your happiest day at work should include one of your greatest professional successes, and how it made you feel. Stay focused on what you accomplished, and be sure to elaborate on how rewarding or satisfying the achievement was for you.

36: Tell me about your worst day at work.

Answer:

It may have been the worst day ever because of all the mistakes you made, or because you'd just had a huge argument with your best friend, but make sure to keep this answer professionally focused. Try to use an example in which something uncontrollable happened in the workplace (such as an important member of a team quit unexpectedly, which ruined your team's meeting with a client), and focus on the frustration of not being in control of the situation. Keep this answer brief, and be sure to end with a reflection on what you learned from the day.

37: What are you passionate about?

Answer:

Keep this answer professionally-focused where possible, but it may also be appropriate to discuss personal issues you are passionate about as well (such as the environment or volunteering at a soup kitchen). Stick to issues that are non-controversial, and allow your passion to shine through as you explain what inspires you about the topic and how you stay actively engaged in it. Additionally, if you choose a personal passion, make sure it is one that does not detract from your availability to work or to be productive.

38: What is the piece of criticism you receive most often?

Answer:

An honest, candid answer to this question can greatly impress an interviewer (when, of course, it is coupled with an explanation of what you're doing to improve), but make sure the criticism is something minimal or unrelated to your career.

39: What type of work environment do you succeed the most in?

Answer:

Be sure to research the company and the specific position before heading into the interview. Tailor your response to fit the job you'd be working in, and explain why you enjoy that type of environment over others. However, it's also extremely important to be adaptable, so remain flexible to other environments as well.

40: Are you an emotional person?

Answer:

It's best to focus on your positive emotions – passion, happiness, motivations – and to stay away from other extreme emotions that may cause you to appear unbalanced. While you want to display your excitement for the job, be sure to remain level-headed and cool at all times, so that the interviewer knows you're not the type of person who lets emotions take you over and get in the way of your work.

41: What is the best way for a company to advertise?

Answer:

If you're going for a position in any career other than marketing, this question is probably intended to demonstrate your ability to think critically and to provide reflective support for your answers. As such, the particular method you choose is not so important as why you've chosen it. For example, word of mouth advertising is important because customers will inherently trust the source, and social media advertising is important as it reaches new customers quickly and cheaply.

42: Is it better to gain a new customer or to keep an old one?

Answer:

In almost every case, it is better to keep an old customer, and it's important that you are able to articulate why this is. First, new customers generally cost companies more than retaining old ones does, and new customers are more likely to switch to a different company. Additionally, keeping old customers is a great way to provide a stable backbone for the company, as well as to also gain new customers as they are likely to recommend your company to friends.

43: What is the best way to win clients from competitors?

Answer:

There are many schools of thought on the best way to win clients from competitors, and unless you know that your interviewer adheres to a specific thought or practice, it's best to keep this question general. Rather than using absolute language, focus on the benefits of one or two strategies and show a clear, critical understanding of how these ways can succeed in a practical application.

44: How do you feel about companies monitoring internet usage?

Answer:

Generally speaking, most companies will monitor some degree of internet usage over their employees – and during an interview is not the best time to rebel against this practice. Instead, focus on positive aspects such as the way it can lead to increased productivity for some employees who may be easily lost in the world of resourceful information available to them.

45: What is your first impression of our company?

Answer:

Obviously, this should be a positive answer! Pick out a couple key components of the company's message or goals that you especially identify with or that pertain to your experience, and discuss why you believe these missions are so important.

46: Tell me about your personal philosophy on business.

Answer:

Your personal philosophy on business should be well-thought out, and in line with the missions and objectives of the company. Stay focused on positive aspects such as the service it can provide, and the lessons people gain in business, and offer insight as to where your philosophy has come from.

47: What's most important in a business model: sales, customer service, marketing, management, etc.?

Answer:

For many positions, it may be a good strategy to tailor this answer to the type of field you're working in, and to explain why that aspect of business is key. However, by explaining that each aspect is integral to the function as a whole, you can display a greater sense of business savvy to the interviewer and may stand out in his or her mind as a particularly aware candidate.

48: How do you keep up with news and emerging trends in the field?

Answer:

The interviewer wants to see that you are aware of what's currently going on in your field. It is important that your education does not stop after college, and the most successful candidates will have a list of resources they regularly turn to already in place, so that they may stay aware and engaged in developing trends.

49: Would you have a problem adhering to company policies on social media?

Answer:

Social media concerns in the workplace have become a greater issue, and many companies now outline policies for the use of social media. Interviewers will want to be assured that you won't have a problem adhering to company standards, and that you will maintain a consistent, professional image both in the office and online.

50: Tell me about one of the greatest problems facing *X industry* today.

Answer:

If you're involved in your career field, and spend time on your own studying trends and new developments, you should be able to display an awareness of both problems and potential solutions coming up in the industry. Research some of the latest news before heading into the interview, and be prepared to discuss current events thoroughly.

51: What do you think it takes to be successful in our company?

Answer:

Research the company prior to the interview. Be aware of the company's mission and main objectives, as well as some of the biggest names in the company, and also keep in mind how they achieved success. Keep your answer focused on specific objectives you could reach in order to help the company achieve its goals.

52: What is your favorite part of working in this career field?

Answer:

This question is an opportunity to discuss some of your favorite aspects of the job, and to highlight why you are a great candidate for the particular position. Choose elements of the work you enjoy that are related to what you would do if hired for the position. Remember to remain enthusiastic and excited for the opportunities you could attain in the job.

53: What do you see happening to your career in the next 10 years?

Answer:

If you're plugged in to what's happening in your career now, and are making an effort to stay abreast of emerging trends in your field, you should be able to offer the interviewer several predictions as to where your career or field may be heading. This insight and level of awareness shows a level of dedication and interest that is important to employers.

54: Describe a time when you communicated a difficult or complicated idea to a coworker.

Answer:

Start by explaining the idea briefly to the interviewer, and then give an overview of why it was necessary to break it down further to the coworker. Finally, explain the idea in succinct steps, so the interviewer can see your communication abilities and skill in simplification.

55: What situations do you find it difficult to communicate in?

Answer:

Even great communicators will often find particular situations that are more difficult to communicate effectively in, so don't be afraid to answer this question honestly. Be sure to explain why the particular situation you name is difficult for you, and try to choose an uncommon answer such as language barrier or in time of hardship, rather than a situation such as speaking to someone of higher authority.

56: What are the key components of good communication?

Answer:

Some of the components of good communication include an environment that is free from distractions, feedback from the listener, and revision or clarification from the speaker when necessary. Refer to basic communication models where necessary, and offer to go through a role-play sample with the interviewer in order to show your skills.

57: Tell me about a time when you solved a problem through communication?

Answer:

Solving problems through communication is key in the business world, so choose a specific situation from your previous job in which you navigated a messy situation by communicating effectively through the conflict. Explain the basis of the situation, as well as the communication steps you took, and end with a discussion of why communicating through the problem was so important to its resolution.

58: Tell me about a time when you had a dispute with another employee. How did you resolve the situation?

Answer:

Make sure to use a specific instance, and explain step-by-step the scenario, what you did to handle it, and how it was finally resolved. The middle step, how you handled the dispute, is clearly the most definitive – describe the types of communication you used, and how you used compromise to reach a decision. Conflict resolution is an important skill for any employee to have, and is one that interviewers will search for to determine both how likely you are to be involved in disputes, and how likely they are to be forced to become involved in the dispute if one arises.

59: Do you build relationships quickly with people, or take more time to get to know them?

Answer:

Either of these options can display good qualities, so determine which style is more applicable to you. Emphasize the steps you take in relationship-building over the particular style, and summarize briefly why this works best for you.

60: Describe a time when you had to work through office politics to solve a problem.

Answer:

Try to focus on the positives in this question, so that you can use the situation to your advantage. Don't portray your previous employer negatively, and instead use a minimal instance (such as paperwork or a single individual), to highlight how you worked through a specific instance resourcefully. Give examples of communication skills or problem-solving you used in order to achieve a resolution.

61: Tell me about a time when you persuaded others to take on a difficult task?

Answer:

This question is an opportunity to highlight both your leadership and communication skills. While the specific situation itself is important to offer as background, focus on how you were able to persuade the others, and what tactics worked the best.

62: Tell me about a time when you successfully persuaded a group to accept your proposal.

Answer:

This question is designed to determine your resourcefulness and your communication skills. Explain the ways in which you took into account different perspectives within the group, and created a presentation that would be appealing and convincing to all members. Additionally, you can pump up the proposal itself by offering details about it that show how well-executed it was.

63: Tell me about a time when you had a problem with another person, that, in hindsight, you wished you had handled differently.

Answer:

The key to this question is to show your capabilities of reflection and your learning process. Explain the situation, how you handled it at the time, what the outcome of the situation was, and finally, how you would handle it now. Most importantly, tell the interviewer why you would handle it differently now – did your previous solution create stress on the relationship with the other person, or do you wish that you had stood up more for what you wanted? While you shouldn't elaborate on how poorly you handled the situation before, the most important thing is to show that you've grown and reached a deeper level of understanding as a result of the conflict.

64: Tell me about a time when you negotiated a conflict between other employees.

Answer:

An especially important question for those interviewing for a supervisory role – begin with a specific situation, and explain how you communicated effectively to each individual. For example, did you introduce a compromise? Did you make an executive decision? Or, did you perform as a mediator and encourage the employees to reach a conclusion on their own?

65: Why would your skills be a good match with X *objective* of our company?

Answer:

If you've researched the company before the interview, answering this question should be no problem. Determine several of the company's main objectives, and explain how specific skills that you have are conducive to them. Also, think about ways that your experience and skills can translate to helping the company expand upon these objectives, and to reach further goals. If your old company had a similar objective, give a specific example of how you helped the company to meet it.

66: What do you think this job entails?

Answer:

Make sure you've researched the position well before heading into the interview. Read any and all job descriptions you can find (at best, directly from the employer's website or job posting), and make note of key duties, responsibilities, and experience required. Few things are less impressive to an interviewer than a candidate who has no idea what sort of job they're actually being interviewed for.

67: Is there anything else about the job or company you'd like to know?

Answer:

If you have learned about the company beforehand, this is a great opportunity to show that you put in the effort to study before the interview. Ask questions about the company's mission in relation to current industry trends, and engage the interviewer in interesting, relevant conversation. Additionally, clear up anything else you need to know about the specific position before leaving – so that if the interviewer calls with an offer, you'll be prepared to answer.

68: Are you the best candidate for this position?

Answer:

Yes! Offer specific details about what makes you qualified for this position, and be sure to discuss (and show) your unbridled passion and enthusiasm for the new opportunity, the job, and the company.

69: How did you prepare for this interview?

Answer:

The key part of this question is to make sure that you have prepared! Be sure that you've researched the company, their objectives, and their services prior to the interview, and know as much about the specific position as you possibly can. It's also helpful to learn about the company's history and key players in the current organization.

70: If you were hired here, what would you do on your first day?

Answer:

While many people will answer this question in a boring fashion, going through the standard first day procedures, this question is actually a great chance for you to show the interviewer why you will make a great hire. In addition to things like going through training or orientation, emphasize how much you would enjoy meeting your supervisors and coworkers, or how you would spend a lot of the day asking questions and taking in all of your new surroundings.

71: Have you viewed our company's website?

Answer:

Clearly, you should have viewed the company's website and done some preliminary research on them before coming to the interview. If for some reason you did not, do not say that you did, as the interviewer may reveal you by asking a specific question about it. If you did look at the company's website, this is an appropriate time to bring up something you saw there that was of particular interest to you, or a value that you especially supported.

72: How does *X experience* on your resume relate to this position?

Answer:

Many applicants will have some bit of experience on their resume that does not clearly translate to the specific job in question. However, be prepared to be asked about this type of seemingly-irrelevant experience, and have a response prepared that takes into account similar skill sets or training that the two may share.

73: Why do you want this position?

Answer:

Keep this answer focused positively on aspects of this specific job that will allow you to further your skills, offer new experience, or that will be an opportunity for you to do something that you particularly enjoy. Don't tell the interviewer that you've been looking for a job for a long time, or that the pay is very appealing, or you will appear unmotivated and opportunistic.

74: How is your background relevant to this position?

Answer:

Ideally, this should be obvious from your resume. However, in instances where your experience is more loosely-related to the position, make sure that you've researched the job and company well before the interview. That way, you can intelligently relate the experience and skills that you do have, to similar skills that would be needed in the new position. Explain specifically how your skills will translate, and use words to describe your background such as "preparation" and "learning." Your prospective position should be described as an "opportunity" and a chance for "growth and development."

75: How do you feel about *X mission* of our company?

Answer:

It's important to have researched the company prior to the interview – and if you've done so, this question won't catch you off guard. The best answer is one that is simple, to the point, and shows knowledge of the mission at hand. Offer a few short statements as to why you believe in the mission's importance, and note that you would be interested in the chance to work with a company that supports it.

And Finally Good Luck!

INDEX

Java/J2EE Interview Questions

Architectures and Protocols

and user interface?

25: What are the advantages and disadvantages of HTTP protocol?

26: Explain JRMP.

27: What are the advantages and disadvantages of CORBA?

28: Explain DCOM.

29: Explain the capabilities of J2EE architecture.

30: Explain System architecture and Reference architecture.

Applicability and Best Practices

31: Explain the best practices to be followed for better performance

32: How do Struts, Spring, and Hibernate help improve performance?

33: How does Garbage Collection help in better performance?

34: Explain Best Practice.

35: Explain the J2EE tiers.

36: What are the best practices to be followed in the presentation layer?

37: What type of components is used in MVC?

38: What are the requirements that a J2EE system must possess to operate in a global economy?

39: What are the best practices to be followed in DAO?

40: Explain Guideline.

41: What are the best practices to be followed in VO?

42: What are the best practices to be followed in session bean facade?

43: What are the benefits of Model View Controller (MVC)?

44: What are the design problems with MVC?

45: Explain the applicability of MVC.

46: Explain the importance of patterns in J2EE framework.

47: Explain Framework patterns.

48: What are the activities of a deployer?

49: What are the patterns that belong to Integration Tier?

50: Explain Presentation Tier patterns.

51: Explain Business Tier patterns.

Servlets

78: How do you send compressed web pages from Servlet to browser?

79: Explain status codes.

80: Explain the meaning of status code 200 and 404.

81: Explain sendRedirect method.

82: How can we display an error message if a particular page or servlet is not available?

83: What are the methods used to set header values?

84: What are the values that can be retrieved from the header?

85: Explain MIME.

86: Explain the most widely used MIME types.

87: What is a Cookie?

88: What are the advantages of Cookies?

89: How can you set and get a cookie?

90: What are the disadvantages of Cookies?

91: What are the options to track visitors browsing a web page?

92: How can you store and retrieve a value from session?

93: Explain Session tracking.

JSP

94: Why should we avoid scriptlets in JSP?

95: What do you mean by JSP Compilation?

96: What are the life-cycle methods in JSP?

97: How to set and delete cookies from inside a JSP page?

98: What is the purpose of JSP?

99: What are JSP constructs?

100: What are scripting elements?

101: What are the most widely used JSP objects?

102: Explain how to get parameter value in JSP.

103: How to display the dynamic parameter value in JSP?

104: What are the predefined JSP objects other than request, response, session, and out?

EJB

component?

130: What are the types of Enterprise Java Beans?

131: Explain EJBHome interface.

132: Explain EJBObject interface.

133: What is deployment descriptor?

134: What is a bean class?

135: Explain context object.

136: What are the types of session beans?

137: What are the methods of remote interfaces?

138: What are the methods of home interfaces?

139: What are the services provided by the local and remote interfaces?

140: Explain how a session bean is exposed to the client.

141: Explain local client.

142: Explain remote client.

143: When we have to use EJB?

144: How to manage bean persistence?

145: Explain bean managed persistence.

146: Explain container managed persistence.

147: Explain how will you create home interface of a stateless session bean.

148: Explain how will you create remote interface of a stateless session bean.

149: Explain InitialContext.

150: What are the benefits of pooling in EJB container?

151: What is the benefit of using DAO between entity bean and data resource?

152: Explain the role of EJB container in managing entity bean life cycle.

153: What are the benefits of CMP?

154: What are the benefits of BMP?

155: What are the drawbacks of CMP?

156: What are the drawbacks of BMP?

Internationalization and Localization

183: What are the characteristics of internationalized application?

184: What are the elements through which a locale is identified?

185: Is it possible to use java.util package for Localization?

186: Explain ResourceBundle.

187: What are the features of ResourceBundle?

188: Explain Character Sets.

189: Explain Unicode.

190: Explain UTF.

191: Explain Collation and Collator.

192: What are the attributes used in JSP to control encoding?

193: Explain Format class.

194: What are the aspects of the application that have to be varied if they have to be deployed in different locales?

195: What are the font names and font styles supported in Java?

196: What are the features of java used to create internationalized application?

197: What are the subclasses of Format class?

198: Explain why UTF-8 is considered the best encoding choice?

199: What are the approaches for localizing JSP pages?

200: What are the advantages of creating JSP for each locale?

201: Explain I18N and L10N.

202: Explain InputStreamReader.

203: Explain OutputStreamWriter.

204: What are the advantages and disadvantages of using ResourceBundle in JSP?

Design Patterns

205: How do you make sure a class is Singleton? What is the disadvantage of a singleton class?

206: What are Design Patterns?

207: What are the benefits of Design Patterns?

Messaging

236: Explain JMS.

237: What are the message models supported by JMS?

238: What are the benefits of synchronous messaging?

239: What are the benefits of asynchronous messaging?

240: What are the scenarios for which we go for asynchronous messaging?

241: What are the advantages of JMS?

242: What are the components of JMS?

243: How are exceptions handled in JMS?

244: How are messages acknowledged in JMS?

245: Explain the message headers of JMS.

246: What are the body formats of JMS?

247: What are the types of administered objects in JMS?

248: What are the objects used to receive and create messages in JMS?

249: Explain Message Consumer.

250: Explain Message Producer.

251: Explain Message Selector.

252: Explain Message Listener.

253: What are the classes, interfaces, and steps required for PTP communication?

254: What are the classes, interfaces, and steps required for Pub/Sub communication?

255: Explain MDB.

Security and Legacy Connectivity

256: What are the various security threats to enterprise resources?

257: Explain Authentication and Authorization.

258: Explain some of the security packages available in Java.

259: What are the actions performed by Java Security Manger in Applets?

260: What are the security restrictions in Java applets?

261: What are the system properties that applet cannot read?

HR Questions

1: Tell me about a time when you didn't meet a deadline.

2: How do you eliminate distractions while working?

3: Tell me about a time when you worked in a position with a weekly or monthly quota to meet. How often were you successful?

4: Tell me about a time when you met a tough deadline, and how you were able to complete it.

5: How do you stay organized when you have multiple projects on your plate?

6: How much time during your work day do you spend on "auto-pilot?"

7: How do you handle deadlines?

8: Tell me about your personal problem-solving process.

9: What sort of things at work can make you stressed?

10: What do you look like when you are stressed about something? How do you solve it?

11: Can you multi-task?

12: How many hours per week do you work?

13: How many times per day do you check your email?

14: What has been your biggest success?

15: What motivates you?

16: What do you do when you lose motivation?

17: What do you like to do in your free time?

18: What sets you apart from other workers?

19: Why are you the best candidate for that position?

20: What does it take to be successful?

21: What would be the biggest challenge in this position for you?

22: Would you describe yourself as an introvert or an extrovert?

23: What are some positive character traits that you don't possess?

24: What is the greatest lesson you've ever learned?

25: Have you ever been in a situation where one of your strengths became a weakness in an alternate setting?

53: What do you see happening to your career in the next 10 years?

54: Describe a time when you communicated a difficult or complicated idea to a coworker.

55: What situations do you find it difficult to communicate in?

56: What are the key components of good communication?

57: Tell me about a time when you solved a problem through communication?

58: Tell me about a time when you had a dispute with another employee. How did you resolve the situation?

59: Do you build relationships quickly with people, or take more time to get to know them?

60: Describe a time when you had to work through office politics to solve a problem.

61: Tell me about a time when you persuaded others to take on a difficult task?

62: Tell me about a time when you successfully persuaded a group to accept your proposal.

63: Tell me about a time when you had a problem with another person, that, in hindsight, you wished you had handled differently.

64: Tell me about a time when you negotiated a conflict between other employees.

65: Why would your skills be a good match with X objective of our company?

66: What do you think this job entails?

67: Is there anything else about the job or company you'd like to know?

68: Are you the best candidate for this position?

69: How did you prepare for this interview?

70: If you were hired here, what would you do on your first day?

71: Have you viewed our company's website?

72: How does X experience on your resume relate to this position?

73: Why do you want this position?

74: How is your background relevant to this position?

75: How do you feel about X mission of our company?

Some of the following titles might also be handy:

1. NET Interview Questions You'll Most Likely Be Asked
2. 200 Interview Questions You'll Most Likely Be Asked
3. Access VBA Programming Interview Questions You'll Most Likely Be Asked
4. Adobe ColdFusion Interview Questions You'll Most Likely Be Asked
5. Advanced Excel Interview Questions You'll Most Likely Be Asked
6. Advanced JAVA Interview Questions You'll Most Likely Be Asked
7. Advanced SAS Interview Questions You'll Most Likely Be Asked
8. AJAX Interview Questions You'll Most Likely Be Asked
9. Algorithms Interview Questions You'll Most Likely Be Asked
10. Android Development Interview Questions You'll Most Likely Be Asked
11. Ant & Maven Interview Questions You'll Most Likely Be Asked
12. Apache Web Server Interview Questions You'll Most Likely Be Asked
13. Artificial Intelligence Interview Questions You'll Most Likely Be Asked
14. ASP.NET Interview Questions You'll Most Likely Be Asked
15. Automated Software Testing Interview Questions You'll Most Likely Be Asked
16. Base SAS Interview Questions You'll Most Likely Be Asked
17. BEA WebLogic Server Interview Questions You'll Most Likely Be Asked
18. C & C++ Interview Questions You'll Most Likely Be Asked
19. C# Interview Questions You'll Most Likely Be Asked
20. C++ Internals Interview Questions You'll Most Likely Be Asked
21. CCNA Interview Questions You'll Most Likely Be Asked
22. Cloud Computing Interview Questions You'll Most Likely Be Asked
23. Computer Architecture Interview Questions You'll Most Likely Be Asked
24. Computer Networks Interview Questions You'll Most Likely Be Asked
25. Core JAVA Interview Questions You'll Most Likely Be Asked
26. Data Structures & Algorithms Interview Questions You'll Most Likely Be Asked
27. Data WareHousing Interview Questions You'll Most Likely Be Asked
28. EJB 3.0 Interview Questions You'll Most Likely Be Asked
29. Entity Framework Interview Questions You'll Most Likely Be Asked
30. Fedora & RHEL Interview Questions You'll Most Likely Be Asked
31. GNU Development Interview Questions You'll Most Likely Be Asked
32. Hibernate, Spring & Struts Interview Questions You'll Most Likely Be Asked
33. HTML, XHTML and CSS Interview Questions You'll Most Likely Be Asked
34. HTML5 Interview Questions You'll Most Likely Be Asked
35. IBM WebSphere Application Server Interview Questions You'll Most Likely Be Asked
36. iOS SDK Interview Questions You'll Most Likely Be Asked
37. Java / J2EE Design Patterns Interview Questions You'll Most Likely Be Asked
38. Java / J2EE Interview Questions You'll Most Likely Be Asked
39. Java Messaging Service Interview Questions You'll Most Likely Be Asked
40. JavaScript Interview Questions You'll Most Likely Be Asked
41. JavaServer Faces Interview Questions You'll Most Likely Be Asked
42. JDBC Interview Questions You'll Most Likely Be Asked
43. jQuery Interview Questions You'll Most Likely Be Asked
44. JSP-Servlet Interview Questions You'll Most Likely Be Asked
45. JUnit Interview Questions You'll Most Likely Be Asked
46. Linux Commands Interview Questions You'll Most Likely Be Asked
47. Linux Interview Questions You'll Most Likely Be Asked
48. Linux System Administrator Interview Questions You'll Most Likely Be Asked
49. Mac OS X Lion Interview Questions You'll Most Likely Be Asked
50. Mac OS X Snow Leopard Interview Questions You'll Most Likely Be Asked

51. Microsoft Access Interview Questions You'll Most Likely Be Asked
52. Microsoft Excel Interview Questions You'll Most Likely Be Asked
53. Microsoft Powerpoint Interview Questions You'll Most Likely Be Asked
54. Microsoft Word Interview Questions You'll Most Likely Be Asked
55. MySQL Interview Questions You'll Most Likely Be Asked
56. NetSuite Interview Questions You'll Most Likely Be Asked
57. Networking Interview Questions You'll Most Likely Be Asked
58. OOPS Interview Questions You'll Most Likely Be Asked
59. Operating Systems Interview Questions You'll Most Likely Be Asked
60. Oracle DBA Interview Questions You'll Most Likely Be Asked
61. Oracle E-Business Suite Interview Questions You'll Most Likely Be Asked
62. ORACLE PL/SQL Interview Questions You'll Most Likely Be Asked
63. Perl Programming Interview Questions You'll Most Likely Be Asked
64. PHP Interview Questions You'll Most Likely Be Asked
65. PMP Interview Questions You'll Most Likely Be Asked
66. Python Interview Questions You'll Most Likely Be Asked
67. RESTful JAVA Web Services Interview Questions You'll Most Likely Be Asked
68. Ruby Interview Questions You'll Most Likely Be Asked
69. Ruby on Rails Interview Questions You'll Most Likely Be Asked
70. SAP ABAP Interview Questions You'll Most Likely Be Asked
71. SAP HANA Interview Questions You'll Most Likely Be Asked
72. SAS Programming Guidelines Interview Questions You'll Most Likely Be Asked
73. Selenium Testing Tools Interview Questions You'll Most Likely Be Asked
74. Silverlight Interview Questions You'll Most Likely Be Asked
75. Software Repositories Interview Questions You'll Most Likely Be Asked
76. Software Testing Interview Questions You'll Most Likely Be Asked
77. SQL Server Interview Questions You'll Most Likely Be Asked
78. Tomcat Interview Questions You'll Most Likely Be Asked
79. UML Interview Questions You'll Most Likely Be Asked
80. Unix Interview Questions You'll Most Likely Be Asked
81. UNIX Shell Programming Interview Questions You'll Most Likely Be Asked
82. VB.NET Interview Questions You'll Most Likely Be Asked
83. Windows Server 2008 R2 Interview Questions You'll Most Likely Be Asked
84. XLXP, XSLT, XPATH, XFORMS & XQuery Interview Questions You'll Most Likely Be Asked
85. XML Interview Questions You'll Most Likely Be Asked

For complete list visit

www.vibrantpublishers.com

Lightning Source UK Ltd.
Milton Keynes UK
UKOW06f1847180617
303618UK00021B/457/P

9 781946 383235